The Civil War Soldiers and Civilians

Teachers Guide

A Supplemental Teaching Unit
from the Records of the National Archives

NATIONAL
ARCHIVES

National Archives Trust Fund Board
National Archives and Records Administration

A B C ◉ C L I O

ABC – CLIO, Inc
130 Cremona Drive, P.O. Box 1911
Santa Barbara, CA 93116-1911
ISBN 1-57607-782-9

Other Units in this Series:

Photographs used as illustrations on the cover and throughout this book are held in the National Archives and Records Administration. To access these and thousands more like them, visit the National Archives Web site at **www.nara.gov**.

Table of Contents

THE CONSCRIPT BILL!
HOW TO AVOID IT!!
U. S. NAVY.
1,000 MEN WANTED, FOR 12 MONTHS!

Seamen's Pay, - - - - - - - $18.00 per month.
Ordinary Seamen's Pay, - - - - 14.00 " "
Landsmen's Pay, - - - - - - 12.00 " "
$1.50 extra per month to all, Grog Money.

$50,000,000 PRIZES!

Already captured, a large share of which is awarded to Ships Crews. The laws for the distributing of Prize money carefully protects the rights of all the captors.

PETTY OFFICERS,—PROMOTION.—Seamen have a chance for promotion to the offices of Master at Arms, Boatswain's Mates, Quarter Gunners, Captain of Tops, Forecastle, Holds, After-Guard, &c.
Landsmen may be advanced to Armorers, Armorers' Mates, Carpenter's Mates, Sailmakers' Mates, Painters, Coopers, &c.
PAY OF PETTY OFFICERS.—From $20.00 to $45.00 per month.
CHANCES FOR WARRANTS, BOUNTIES AND MEDALS OF HONOR.—All those who distinguish themselves in battle or by extraordinary heroism, may be promoted to forward Warrant Officers or Acting Masters' Mates,—and upon their promotion receive a guaranty of $100, with a medal of honor from their country.
All who wish may leave HALF PAY with their families, to commence from date of enlistment.
Minors must have a written consent, sworn to before a Justice of the Peace.

For further information apply to U. S. NAVAL RENDEZVOUS,
E. Y. BUTLER, U. S. N. Recruiting Officer,
No. 14 FRONT STREET, SALEM, MASS.

FROM WRIGHT & POTTER'S BOSTON PRINTING ESTABLISHMENT, No. 4 SPRING LANE, CORNER OF DEVONSHIRE STREET.

Foreword

The National Archives and Records Service is responsible for the preservation and use of the permanently valuable records of the federal government. These materials provide evidence of the activities of the government from 1774 to the present in the form of written and printed documents, maps and posters, sound recordings, photographs, films, and computer tapes. These rich archival sources are useful to all: federal officials seeking information on past government activities, citizens needing data for use in legal matters, historians interpreting the past, journalists researching stories, students preparing term papers, and persons tracing their ancestry or satisfying their curiosity about particular historical events. The National Archives serves as the nation's memory for a multitude of purposes.

As part of the continuing effort to make these records available to the public in forms most appropriate to its needs, our Office of Educational Programs began in 1970 a program designed to introduce these vast resources to secondary school students. School classes visiting the Archives were given the opportunity to work with archival materials as historians use them. Staff members developed activities to engage students in examining and interpreting original sources; both teachers and students responded enthusiastically. As a result of this success, the National Archives devised a plan to reach larger numbers of students across the nation by publishing a series of supplementary teaching units from National Archives sources. This particular unit, *The Civil War: Soldiers and Civilians*, is the fourth in the series. We hope that these materials will bring you and your students closer to the pleasures and the perils of working with primary sources and will enhance your classroom program.

JAMES E. O'NEILL
Acting Archivist of the United States
1980

...to bring you and your students the excitement and satisfaction of working with primary sources and to enhance your instructional program.

*P*reface

◆ This unit is made up of 5 exercises.

◆ Each exercise includes reproductions of documents from the National Archives and suggests classroom activities based on these documents.

The Civil War: Soldiers and Civilians is a teaching unit designed to supplement your students' study of the Civil War. The unit is made up of five exercises that relate to military and civilian life. Each exercise uses reproductions of documents from the National Archives and suggests classroom activities based on these documents. The documents include letters, photographs, patent drawings, maps, and other documents. Students practice the historian's skills as they complete exercises using these documents to gather information, identify points of view, evaluate evidence, form hypotheses, and draw conclusions.

The documents in this unit do not reflect every topic usually included in a history or government textbook. In some instances, the federal government had no interest in or authority over a given event and therefore created no records on it. In other cases, documents in the National Archives on several historic topics proved to be difficult to use in the classroom due to problems of legibility, length, or format.

National Archives education specialists Michael Hedges and Nadine Smith and Academic and Curricular Programs Director Elsie Freeman Finch developed this publication. We are pleased to issue a revised and updated set of these documentary teaching materials.

WYNELL B. SCHAMEL
LEE ANN POTTER
Education Specialists
2001

The Civil War: Soldiers and Civilians
is a teaching unit designed to supplement
your students' study of the Civil War.

Acknowledgments

Many people helped in the original production of this unit. They included National Archives staff members Mary Alexander, Shelby Bale, Blaine T. Bentley, Stuart Butler, Marilyn Childress, Elizabeth Epps, Bill Leary, Deloris Lott, Kathryn Gent, Nancy Malan, Robert Matchette, George Perros, John Rumbarger, Richard Smith, J. Samuel Walker, and Richard Wood.

Special thanks go to Virginia Cardwell Purdy, formerly Director of the Education Division, Office of Educational Programs, National Archives and Records Service, whose imagination sparked the project. Dale Floyd and Michael Musick, National Archives archivists, and Leslie Rowland, Director of the Freedmen and Southern Society publication project, reviewed the unit for historical content. Professor Thomas Weinland, School of Education, University of Connecticut, reviewed it for instructional content.

During the republication process, we were ably assisted by George Mason University intern Adam Jevec; volunteers, Elizabeth S. Lourie, Jane Douma Pearson, and Donald Alderson; and National Archives staff members Michael Hussey, A.J. Daverede, Patrick Osborn, Amy Patterson, Kate Flaherty, Donald Roe, and Charles Mayn.

Publisher's Note

Primary source documents have long been a cornerstone of ABC-CLIO's commitment to producing high-quality, learner-centered history and social studies resources. When our nation's students have the opportunity to interact with the undiluted artifacts of the past, they can better understand the breadth of the human experience and the present state of affairs.

It is with great enthusiasm that we celebrate the release of this series of teaching units designed in partnership with the National Archives—materials that we hope will bring historical context and deeper knowledge to U.S. middle and high school students. Each unit has been revised and updated, including new bibliographic references. Each teaching unit has been correlated to the curriculum standards for the teaching of social studies and history developed by the National Council for the Social Studies and the National Center for History in the Schools.

For more effective use of these teaching units in the classroom, each booklet is accompanied by an interactive CD-ROM which includes exercise worksheets, digital images of original documents, and, for four titles, sound recordings. A videocassette of motion pictures accompanies the teaching unit *The United States At War: 1944*. For those who would like to order facsimiles of primary source documents in their original sizes, or additional titles in this series, we have included an order form to make it easy for you to do so.

The mission of the National Archives is "to ensure ready access to the essential evidence that documents the rights of American citizens, the actions of Federal officials, and the national experience."

These units go a long way toward fulfilling that mission, helping the next generation of American citizens develop a clear understanding of the nation's past and a firm grasp of the role of the individual in guiding the nation's future. ABC-CLIO is honored to be part of this process.

BECKY SNYDER
Publisher & Vice President
ABC-CLIO Schools

The mission of the National Archives is "to ensure ready access to the essential evidence that documents the rights of American citizens, the actions of Federal officials, and the national experience."

Teaching With Documents Curriculum Standards Correlations

The National Council for the Social Studies and the National Center for History in the Schools have developed a set of comprehensive curriculum standards for the teaching of social studies and history. Take a look at how thoroughly the Teaching With Documents series supports the curriculum.

	The Constitution: Evolution of a Government	The Bill of Rights: Evolution of Personal Liberties	The United States Expands West: 1785–1842	Westward Expansion: 1842–1912	The Civil War: Soldiers and Civilians	The Progressive Years: 1898–1917	World War I: The Home Front	The 1920's	The Great Depression and The New Deal World	War II: The Home Front	The United States At War: 1944	The Truman Years: 1945–1953	Peace and Prosperity: 1953–1961
National Council for the Social Studies													
CULTURE—should provide for the study of culture and cultural diversity	•		•	•				•		•			•
TIME, CONTINUITY & CHANGE—should provide for the study of the ways people view themselves in and over time	•	•	•					•	•		•		
PEOPLE, PLACES & ENVIRONMENT—should provide for the study of people, places, and environments	•	•	•	•	•	•	•	•	•		•		•
INDIVIDUAL DEVELOPMENT & IDENTITY—should provide for the study of individual development and identity	•	•		•	•	•	•	•	•			•	•
INDIVIDUALS, GROUPS & INSTITUTIONS—should provide for the study of interactions among individuals, groups, and institutions	•	•	•	•	•	•		•	•		•	•	•
POWER, AUTHORITY & GOVERNANCE—should provide for the study of how structures of power are created and changed	•	•	•	•	•	•		•	•			•	•
PRODUCTION, DISTRIBUTION & CONSUMPTION—should provide for the study of the usage of goods and services	•		•	•		•		•	•				
SCIENCE, TECHNOLOGY & SOCIETY—should provide for the study of relationships among science, technology, and society	•	•	•	•	•	•		•			•	•	•
GLOBAL CONNECTIONS—should provide for the study of global connections and interdependence	•		•			•					•	•	•
CIVIC IDEALS & PRACTICES—should provide for the study of the ideals, principles, and practices of citizenship	•	•				•		•			•		
National Center for History in the Schools													
CHRONOLOGICAL THINKING	•	•	•	•	•	•	•	•	•	•	•	•	•
HISTORICAL COMPREHENSION	•	•	•	•	•	•	•	•	•	•	•	•	•
HISTORICAL ANALYSIS & INTERPRETATION	•	•	•	•	•	•	•	•	•	•	•	•	•
HISTORICAL RESEARCH CAPABILITIES	•	•	•	•	•	•	•	•	•	•	•	•	•
HISTORICAL ISSUES-ANALYSIS & DECISION-MAKING	•	•	•	•	•	•	•	•	•	•	•	•	•

Introduction

This unit contains two elements: 1) a book, which contains a teachers guide and a set of reproductions of print documents, and 2) a CD-ROM, which contains the exercise worksheets from the teachers guide and a set of reproductions of documents in electronic format. In selecting the documents, we applied three standards. First, the documents must be entirely from the holdings of the National Archives and reflect the actions of the federal government or citizens' responses to those actions. Second, most documents must be typical of the hundreds of similar records relating to a particular topic. (Exceptions were made for distinctive or unique documents of compelling historical value.) Third, the documents must be legible and potentially useful for vocabulary development. In selecting documents, we tried to choose those having appeal to young people and their instructors.

UNIT CONTAINS:

◆ **1)** a book, which contains a teachers guide and a set of reproductions of print documents, and

◆ **2)** a CD-ROM, which contains the exercise worksheets from the teachers guide and a set of reproductions of documents in electronic format.

Objectives

We have provided an outline of the general objectives for the unit. You will be able to achieve these objectives by completing several, if not all, of the exercises in the unit. Because each exercise aims to develop skills defined in the general objectives, you may be selective and still develop those skills. In addition, each exercise has its own specific objectives.

Outline

This unit on the Civil War includes five exercises. In choosing topics for the unit, we have sought less to present a balanced range of content than to present topics that offer the maximum potential for developing students' skills. We have avoided writing history as much as possible. Unfortunately, this unit contains more Union records than Confederate — in part because the federal government was better able to preserve its own records than was the newly organized Confederacy, and in part because Confederate records were scattered following the war.

List of Documents

The list of documents gives specific information (e.g., date and name of author) and record group number for each document. Records in the National Archives are arranged in record groups. A typical record group (RG) consists of the records created or accumulated by a department, agency, bureau, or other administrative unit of the federal government. Each record group is identified for retrieval purposes by an arbitrarily assigned record group number; for example, RG 241 (Records of the Patent Office) or RG 77 (Records of the Office of the Chief of Engineers). Complete archival citations of all documents are listed in the appendix, p. 58.

Introductory Exercises

Before starting exercises 1-5, it is important to help students become familiar with documents and their importance to the historian who interprets them and writes historical accounts from them. We suggest that you direct students to do the introductory exercises, which can be used with most documents, wherever they are found. The Written Document Analysis, p. 8, is designed to help students analyze systematically any written document in the unit. The Photograph Analysis, p. 9, can be used for the same purpose with any of the photographs in this unit.

Classroom Exercises

You may choose to use any of the five topics in this unit independently or use them all for a more thorough development of students' analytical skills. The first topic, "Camp Life," contains primary sources in the form of photographs and other visual materials and focuses on visual literacy skills. "Laborers, Contrabands, and Soldiers" shows how blacks contributed in various ways to the Union effort throughout the Civil War. "The Battle of Ball's Bluff" allows for an examination of one particular battle in the Civil War and the reasons for its outcome. "War and Technology" presents documents that raise the question of whether war generates or impedes technological development. The last topic, "Civilians and Government," provides a look at how a civil war affects the lives of citizens and the workings of government.

We recommend that you ask students to keep a notebook for their work if you use more than one of the topics in this unit. This notebook will be useful as a reference for the concluding discussions and, furthermore, will enable students to make comparisons among the topics. You may also wish to collect students' notebooks to evaluate their work.

Within the explanatory material for each of the five exercises in this unit, you will find the following information:

➤ Note to the teacher   ➤ Materials needed

➤ Classroom time required   ➤ Procedures

➤ Objectives (specific)   ➤ Student worksheets

You may choose to combine several exercises on a topic within the unit. In some instances a document is used in more than one exercise when it is appropriate to the skill or content objectives. We encourage you to select and adapt the exercises and documents that best suit your own teaching style.

Ability Levels

As in our other units, we have developed exercises for students of different abilities. For some topics, we have designed two or more procedures, tailored to different student needs. Throughout the unit we have made an effort to provide exercises in which students use a variety of skills, including reading for understanding; interpreting audiovisual materials, posters, cartoons, maps, and photographs; and analyzing petitions, patents, reports, and correspondence. All lessons have procedures for ability levels one, two, and three. Procedures begin with strategies designed for level three students, continue with level two strategies, and conclude with level one strategies. Our definition of student ability at each ability level is as follows:

Level One: Good reading skills, ability to organize and interpret information from several sources with minimal direction from teacher, and ability to complete assignments independently.

Level Two: Average reading skills, ability to organize and interpret information from several sources with general direction from teacher, and ability to complete assignments with some assistance from teacher.

Level Three: Limited reading skills, and ability to organize and interpret information from several sources with step-by-step direction from teacher, and ability to complete assignments with close supervision from teacher.

These ability levels are merely guides. We recognize that you will adapt the exercises to suit your students' needs and your own teaching style.

Time Line

A time line is included for use by your students. Some exercises suggest that students consult the time line, so you may want to reproduce it for each student or display it.

The time line is designed to give students a scale by which to gauge the rise and fall of fortunes in the North and South and to illustrate and explain some of the points raised in this unit. It is not intended to be a comprehensive chronology.

Glossary

We have included a glossary that provides definitions of specialized words or phrases used in the documents as well as some biographical entries and explanations of abbreviations frequently found in the documents. Students should be made aware of more specialized terms that have meaning in general usage other than or in addition to that given in the glossary.

Bibliography

As students work with the documents, they should be assigned appropriate readings from their textbooks and other secondary sources. They should also be encouraged to use the resources of school and public libraries. To guide them, an annotated bibliography appears at the end of the Teachers Guide. The selections were based on their appropriateness to the subject and their general availability through public and school library systems.

General Objectives

Upon successfully completing the exercises in this unit, students should be able to demonstrate the following skills using a single document:

➤ Identify factual evidence
➤ Identify points of view (bias and/or prejudice)
➤ Collect, reorder, and weigh the significance of evidence
➤ Develop defensible inferences, conclusions, and generalizations from factual information

Using several documents from this unit, students should be able to:

➤ Analyze the documents to compare and contrast evidence
➤ Evaluate and interpret evidence drawn from the documents

Outline of Classroom Exercises

The Civil War: Soldiers and Civilians

Exercise 1
Camp Life

Exercise 2
Laborers, Contrabands, and Soldiers

Exercise 3
The Battle of Ball's Bluff

Exercise 4
War and Technology

Exercise 5
Civilians and Government

List of Documents

Following the identifying information for each document reproduced in this unit, we have given the record group (RG) number in which the original can be found. Should you want copies of these documents or wish to refer to them in correspondence with us, give the complete archival citation, which is found in the appendix on page 58. **You may duplicate any of the documents in this unit for use with your students.**

Documents in *The Civil War: Soldiers and Civilians* are taken from the following record groups: Records of the U.S. Senate (RG 46), Records of the Bureau of Ordnance (RG 74), Records of the Office of the Chief of Engineers (RG 77), Records of the Adjutant General's Office, 1780's-1917 (RG 94), War Department Collection of Confederate Records (RG 109), Records of the Office of the Chief Signal Officer (RG 111), Records of the Patent Office (RG 241), and Records of U.S. Army Continental Commands, 1821-1920 (RG 393).

1. Letter to Gen. E. A. Carman from Hugh Garden, May 1, 1896 (RG 94).
2. Photograph by Mathew Brady, "The inside of an officer's quarters during the Civil War," ca. 1860 (RG 111).
3. Photograph by Mathew Brady, "The camp of the 44th New York Volunteer Infantry near Alexandria, Virginia," ca. 1860 (RG 111).
4. Photograph by Mathew Brady, "Camp scene, Army of the Potomac," ca. 1860 (RG 111).
5. Photograph by Mathew Brady, "A group of the 22nd New York State Militia in full dress uniforms, encamped near Harper's Ferry, Virginia," 1862 (RG 111).
6. Photograph by Mathew Brady, "A company of the 44th Indiana Volunteer Infantry taken in camp," ca. 1860 (RG 111).
7. Photograph by Mathew Brady, "Sutler store and soldier customers," ca. 1860 (RG 111).
8. Excerpt from price list of sutler's goods, February 7, 1863 (RG 94).
9. Poster, "The Conscript Bill! How To Avoid It!!," 1863 (RG 45).
10. Photograph, scene on deck of gunboat *Hunchback*, 1864 (RG 111).
11. Petition of Ned Baxter, Samuel Owens, and 43 others to Maj. Gen. Benjamin Butler, September 1864 (RG 393).
12. Photograph by Mathew Brady, "Negro laborers at Alexandria, ca. 1860-1865 (RG 111).
13. Petition of colored citizens of Beaufort, NC, to Maj. Gen. Benjamin Butler, November 20, 1863 (RG 393).
14. Circular, "Colored Soldiers! Equal State Rights! And Monthly Pay With White Men!!," 1863 (RG 94).
15. Petition of officers of Negro troops stationed at Port Helena, AR, to the Senate and House of Representatives, March 1864 (RG 46).
16. Letter to Maj. Gen. Benjamin Butler from Edwin Hinks on the subject of arms, April 29, 1864 (RG 393).
17. Letter to Maj. Gen. Benjamin Butler from Brigadier General Hinks on the subject of retaliation, May 28, 1864 (RG 393).
18. Letter to governor of Massachusetts about equal pay for black troops, November 23, 1863 (RG 94).
19. Letter to General Banks from free colored men of the city of New Orleans, March 11, 1863 (RG 393).
20. Letter to Adjutant General Thomas from Peter Cook, November 7, 1864 (RG 94).
21. Letter to Secretary of War Stanton from Sarah Brown, February 8, 1865 (RG 94).
22. Letter to the President from Mrs. Stevens, June 11, 1865 (RG 94).
23. Letter to Secretary of War Stanton from Peter Peterson, May 24, 1865 (RG 94).
24. Map, "Ball's Bluff, Loudoun County, Va., 1861," (RG 77).

25. Letter to the Secretary of War from Maj. Gen. George McClellan, November 1, 1861 (RG 94).

26. Letter from Charles P. Stone to Col. Hardie, December 2, 1861 (RG 94).

27. Letter to Col. E. D. Townsend from Francis G. Young, October 28, 1861 (RG 94).

28. Excerpt from letter from N. G. Evans, October 31, 1861 (RG 109).

29. Excerpt from letter to Brigadier General Lauder from Edward W. Hinks, October 23, 1861 (RG 94).

30. Patent drawing, R. J. Gatling's "Revolving Battery" (Gun), patented November 4, 1862 (RG 241).

31. Drawing of "Ganster's Percussion Hand Grenade," October 24, 1864 (RG 74).

32. Letter to Comdr. H. G. Wise from William N. Jeffers, October 24, 1864 (RG 74).

33. Letter to Captain Dahlgren from William Mitchell, November 18, 1862 (RG 74).

34. Page 19 of *General Index of Patents*, 1790-1873 (RG 241).

35. Page 22 of *General Index of Patents*, 1790-1873 (RG 241).

36. Excerpt from *Introduction to Medical and Surgical History of the War of the Rebellion*, pp. XXVIII and XXVIX, Washington: Government Printing Office, 1870 (RG 94).

37. Letter from J. Theodore Calhoun, Assistant Surgeon, U.S. Army, August 26, 1863 (R 94).

38. Case history concerning 1ˢᵗ Sgt. George W. Clark, wounded August 30, 1862 (RG 94).

39. Letter to Mr. L. Casella from Lt. Col. John Billings, May 1864 (RG94).

40. Case history concerning Pvt. Philip Fitzsimmons, wounded August 1, 1863 (RG 94).

41. Patent drawing, "E. R. McKean's improved ambulance," October 11, 1864 (RG 241).

42. Patent drawing, T. L. Shaw's aerostation, patented February 10, 1863 (RG 241).

43. Letter regarding the arrest order for H. Lick, October 15, 1863 (RG 109).

44. Letter to Brig. Gen. Boyle from Col. M. M. Bush, June 31, 1863 (RG 109).

45. Arrest order for Henry Buster for "hurrahing for Jeff. Davis," June 21, 1862 (RG 109).

46. Excerpt from "The Rolla Express," October 10, 1863 (RG 109).

47. Excerpt from Proclamation No. 94, President Lincoln suspending the writ of habeas corpus, September 24, 1862 (RG 109).

48. Letter concerning charges against John Bush, December 11, 1863 (RG 109).

49. Letter from W. D. Richardson concerning Joseph and John Hedge[s], November 16, 1864 (RG 109).

50. Letter to Capt. Charles Fletcher from Fannie Dent, December 1864 (RG 109).

51. Letter to Col. Maxwell from Livania Hedges, November 28, 1864 (RG 109).

52. Oath of allegiance of J. P. Bush, March 3, 1862 (RG 109).

53. Letter from C. Brown concerning Mrs. Ann Bush, October 12, 1861 (RG 109).

54. Excerpt from charges and specifications against H. Lick, October 10, 1863 (RG 109).

Introductory Exercises

These exercises introduce students to the general objectives of the unit. They focus students' attention on documents and their importance to historians, who interpret and record the past. We encourage you to use them as opening exercises for this unit.

Written Document Analysis

The Written Document Analysis worksheet helps students to analyze systematically any written document in this unit. In sections 1-5 of the worksheet, students locate basic details within the document. In section 6, students analyze the document more critically as they complete items A-E. There are many possible correct answers to section 6, A-E. We suggest you use document 1 with this worksheet.

Photograph Document Analysis

The Photograph Analysis worksheet helps students to analyze systematically the historical evidence within photographs. It is designed to improve students' ability to use photographs as historical documents. It can be used specifically with exercises 1 and 2.

Written Document Analysis

Worksheet

1. Type of Document (Check one):

   _____ Newspaper   _____ Map   _____ Advertisement

   _____ Letter   _____ Telegram   _____ Congressional record

   _____ Patent   _____ Press release   _____ Census report

   _____ Memorandum   _____ Report   _____ Other

2. Unique Physical Qualities of the Document (check one or more):

   _____ Interesting letterhead   _____ Notations

   _____ Handwritten   _____ "RECEIVED" stamp

   _____ Typed   _____ Other

   _____ Seals

3. Date(s) of Document: _____

4. Author (or creator) of the Document: _____

   Position (Title): _____

5. For What Audience was the Document Written? _____

6. Document Information (There are many possible ways to answer A-E.)

   A. List three things the author said that you think are important:

      1. _____

      2. _____

      3. _____

   B. Why do you think this document was written?

      _____

      _____

   C. What evidence in the document helps you to know why it was written? Quote from the document.

      _____

      _____

   D. List two things the document tells you about life in the United States at the time it was written:

      1. _____

      2. _____

   E. Write a question to the author that is left unanswered by the document:

      _____

      _____

Designed and developed by the education staff of the National Archives and Records Administration, Washington, DC 20408.

Photograph Analysis

Worksheet

Step 1. Observation

A. Study the photograph for 2 minutes. Form an overall impression of the photograph and then examine individual items. Next, divide the photo into quadrants and study each section to see what new details become visible.

B. Use the chart below to list people, objects, and activities in the photograph.

PEOPLE	OBJECTS	ACTIVITIES
_____	_____	_____
_____	_____	_____
_____	_____	_____
_____	_____	_____
_____	_____	_____
_____	_____	_____

Step 2. Inference

Based on what you have observed above, list three things you might infer from this photograph:

1. _____

2. _____

3. _____

Step 3. Questions

A. What questions does this photograph raise in your mind?

_____

_____

B. Where could you find answers to them?

_____

_____

Designed and developed by the education staff of the National Archives and Records Administration, Washington, DC 20408.

Exercise 1
Camp Life

Note to the Teacher:

What was the daily life of a soldier like during the Civil War? A soldier who enlisted in the most aggressive Civil War regiment and participated in all of that regiment's contact with the enemy might still have been under fire only 1 day in 20. This topic considers the time between the battles – a soldier's life in camp.

The documents in this section are largely visual. Students will be introduced to photographs and posters as sources of primary information. They will practice "reading" photographs; that is, scrutinizing them for relevant facts and details. Students will learn that, as with other sources (letters, newspapers, textbooks, etc.), a photograph is one person's interpretation of an event and is therefore slanted. They will also practice drawing inferences about the circumstances existing beyond the camera's lens.

Students should be reminded that the Civil War was the first large scale war that was extensively photographed. Because the photographs contained in this unit are from the Mathew Brady collection, students might be told of Brady's role as a recorder of the Civil War.

Time: 1-3 class periods

Objectives:

- Recognize photographs and other visual materials as primary sources of information.
- Identify details in a photograph and describe their importance to the subject of the photo.
- Recognize that photographs are a reflection of the photographer's perception of an event or scene.
- Describe the differences between photographic data and textual information and how the two sources complement each other.
- State several ways in which photography changed the documentation of public events.
- Describe the recruiting benefits of service in the Navy during the Civil War.
- Describe three elements of the life of a soldier in camp during the Civil War.

Materials Needed:

Documents 2-10
Worksheets A-D
Photograph Analysis worksheet

Procedures:

1. Divide the class into seven groups and distribute a photograph from the group of documents 2-7 and 10 and a copy of the Photograph Analysis worksheet to each group. Allow time for groups working together to complete the worksheet. Based on the information on the worksheets, discuss with the class what the photographs reveal about a soldier's life during the Civil War. At the conclusion of your discussion, consider what information is missing and where it might be found.

2. Divide the classroom into four stations. At the first station, place worksheet A and document 2; at the second station, documents 3-6 and worksheet B; at station three, documents 7 and 8 and worksheet C; and at station 4, worksheet D and documents 9 and 10.

   a. Assign each group to a station.

   b. Allow approximately 1 period to complete 2 of the worksheets. Ask students to record their answers to the worksheets so they can be checked when the exercise is completed.

   c. When a group has completed a worksheet, they should move to the next station, leaving the worksheets and documents for the next group.

   d. At the end of the second class, discuss with the students what conclusions can be drawn about camp life from the documents in this topic.

3. Using document 10, ask students to imagine that they are one of the people in the photograph. Direct students to write a daily log entry or a letter to a friend describing their life aboard ship based on documents 9 and 10. Encourage students to use the details of the two documents as a basis for their efforts. Evaluation of this assignment should be based on how creatively students use the information from the documents.

4. Extended activities:

   a. Assign students to write a research paper on the history of photography, photography in the Civil War, Mathew Brady, Alexander Gardner, or Timothy O'Sullivan.

   b. Ask students to use all the photographs in this unit as the basis for an essay on camp life during the Civil War.

   c. Invite students to use family photographs, old and new, in a phototextual essay about your life or your family's life.

   Note: More than 6,000 photographs taken by Mathew Brady have been digitized by the National Archives and are available online at **www.nara.gov**.

I

Exercise 1: Camp Life
Worksheet A

1. Repeat step one of the Photograph Analysis worksheet to examine document 2.

2. Answer the following questions:

   a. Who occupies this dwelling?

   b. Is the occupant literate? On what do you base your answer?

   c. Is he a member of the cavalry or the infantry? Explain your answer.

   d. Does he belong to the Union or Confederate Army? How do you know?

   e. Is the army on the move or in permanent camp? Cite information in the photo to support your answer.

3. Identify as many objects in the photograph as you can. Tell how they would have been used by a Civil War soldier.

4. What do you think the photographer was attempting to illustrate in the photograph?

Exercise 1: Camp Life

Worksheet B

1. Repeat step one of the Photograph Analysis worksheet to examine documents 3 and 4. For each photograph:

   a. Write a sentence stating the subject of the photo.

   b. Describe the mood or feeling of each photo.

   c. Write a caption that describes the subject of the photo.

2. If you were writing an article on a soldier's camp, which photograph would you use to illustrate it? Why?

3. Repeat step one of the Photograph Analysis worksheet to examine documents 5 and 6.

   a. Compare and contrast the two photos.

   b. How do these documents add to your understanding of camp life during the Civil War?

   c. Why do you think these photographs were taken?

4. Use the Photograph Analysis worksheet to examine a photograph of the Civil War in your textbook. Compare and contrast documents 3-6 with this photo.

Exercise 1: Camp Life

Worksheet C

1. Repeat step one of the Photograph Analysis worksheet to examine document 7. According to the caption in the photograph, the building pictured is a sutler's store – a store in camp where men could buy food and dry goods (see glossary).

2. Answer the following questions:

   a. Would you know what the function of the building was without the caption? Why or why not?

   b. If the photographer wanted to show the variety of goods available at a sutler's store, would this be an effective photograph? Why or why not?

   c. What functions, other than a place to buy goods, were served by the sutler's store? Cite your evidence.

3. Study document 8. What does this document add to the information presented in the photograph?

4. Which of the two documents do you think would be more important in an article about sutlers' stores? In an article about soldiers' lives in camp? Why?

5. Assume the role of a Civil War soldier. Using the two documents, write a diary entry about your visit to a sutler's store.

Exercise 1: Camp Life

Worksheet D

1. Examine document 9 carefully. List the benefits of joining the navy. Which are emphasized? According to the poster artist, what was the single best reason for joining the navy at the time the poster was created?

2. Repeat step one of the Photograph Analysis worksheet to examine document 10. Why do you think there is such a variety of ages among the men aboard ship?

3. Describe the naval recruitment policy using information from the poster and the photograph.

Exercise 2
Laborers, Contrabands, and Soldiers

Note to the Teacher:

From serving as members of a labor force in the first 20 months of the war to fighting as members of special regiments, blacks – both freedmen and runaway slaves – contributed significantly to the Union war effort. This exercise will document the experiences of some of these men. It includes letters from families of freedmen describing problems at home and a letter from an officer of a black regiment requesting the very best arms the country can buy to protect his men from the special dangers they face. Among the dangers were not only the rigors of war that all Civil War soldiers regularly faced, but also the threat of slavery for blacks captured by Confederate troops.

In activity 1 students will read a letter of grievance written by members of a black labor force. Using this letter as the basis for a role-playing activity, students will develop arguments to persuade others in the class to their point of view. In activity 2 students use the photo-reading skills introduced in exercise 1. They will study a photograph and two textual documents to form a hypothesis on the effect of the Civil War on black Americans. Activity 3 is an independent study project in which students read documents about discrimination in the military. They will record evidence of discrimination on a chart to use later in a class discussion or written assignment on the subject.

Students will read letters written by families of the men of the United States Colored Troops (U.S.C.T.) in exercise 4. Working in groups, they will study the hardships that these families endured. Students will share the evidence of the letters within their groups and analyze the chief concerns of each writer.

Records used in this topic are from the Mathew Brady Collection of Civil War Photographs found among Records of the Office of the Chief Signal Officer (RG 111); Records of the Adjutant General's Office, 1780's-1917 (RG 94); Records of U.S. Army Continental Commands, 1821-1920 (RG 393); and Records of the U.S. Senate (RG 46).

Time: 1-3 class periods

Objectives:

- Describe the chief concerns of family members of men belonging to the United States Colored Troops.

- Identify evidence of racial discrimination during the Civil War.

- Develop hypotheses about the effects of the Civil War on black Americans.

Materials Needed:

Documents 11-23
Worksheets E and F
Photograph Analysis worksheet
Glossary
Time Line

Procedures:

1. Duplicate document 11 and worksheet E for each student and distribute them. Students will use these materials to prepare for a role-playing activity.

   a. Allow 10 minutes for students to read the document and complete part A of the worksheet. Discuss with students their responses to question 6 on the worksheet.

   b. Prepare students for the role-playing exercise by having them assume that:
      1) The families of the men are being moved to another location.
      2) Samuel Owens, one of the signers of the letter, refuses to work any longer for the federal government and urges other men to leave with him.
      3) Ned Baxter, another signer of the letter, encourages the men to stay to help the Union cause.

      Remind students that these men have just begun to live as free men, and are no longer the property of white owners.

   c. Direct each student to assume the role of one of the other men of Roanoke Island. To help them do this, ask students to:
      1) Make up a name.
      2) Think about any experiences that may influence personal feelings.
      3) Consider the prospects for the future.

   d. Direct students to use the information in the document to prepare an argument in which they try to persuade other members of the labor force to their point of view. Outline this argument on part B of the worksheet.

   e. Convene a meeting of the men on Roanoke Island to decide whether they will leave or stay to help the Union forces. After the arguments are presented, students should vote to leave or stay, basing their votes on how skillfully and accurately the information from the document has been used to develop the arguments.

   f. Collect the worksheets to evaluate the outline of students' arguments and to review their answers to part A.

2. Duplicate the Photograph Analysis worksheet and document 12 for each student. Reproduce enough copies of documents 11 and 13 to circulate among the students.

   a. Give each student a copy of document 12 and the Photograph Analysis worksheet. Tell students that the photograph is from the Mathew Brady Collection of Civil War photographs. Allow students time to study the photograph and complete the worksheet.

   b. Circulate copies of documents 11 and 13. Ask students to read these and determine how they supplement the photograph. How are the three documents similar? How do they differ? How might these three documents be used together?

2

c. Ask students to form a hypothesis about the effect of the Civil War on black Americans using the three documents.

d. Place their hypotheses on the blackboard and discuss them. Consider how you might test these hypotheses.

e. If exercise 1 has been completed, discuss with students how the documents in this exercise add to what they know about the role of blacks in the Civil War.

f. Collect the worksheets to review students' work.

3. Duplicate documents 14-18 and make a document file with which students can work independently. If your class is large you may want to reproduce a set of documents 14-18 to set up more than one file. Make the document file available to the students as a resource center where they can work at their own pace.

Tell the class that document 14 includes information on protection of "colored troops." During the Civil War, prisoners of war on both sides were imprisoned; however, they were not generally used as laborers by their captors. In 1863, in response both to the enlistment of black troops by the Union and fear of slave uprisings, the Confederate Congress threatened to severely punish the officers of black troops and to enslave the black soldiers. As a result, Lincoln issued General Order 233, mentioned in the document. However, neither the North nor the South officially followed through with their threats.

a. Direct the students to read the documents for evidence of discrimination during the Civil War. They should note such evidence on a chart set up in this way:

DOCUMENT NUMBER/WRITER

Cite any reference from the documents about:

    Pay

    Equipment

    Service Assignments

    Promotions

    "Colored Troops" as Prisoners of War

b. When the charts are complete, conduct a discussion about the status of black soldiers during the Civil War.

c. Assign students to use the information in the documents to write one of the following:

    1) A journal entry of a member of the U.S.C.T.

    2) A letter from a U.S.C.T. soldier to a son who wants to enlist.

    3) An account of the role of black soldiers for either an abolitionist or Southern newspaper.

4. Divide your class into groups with four students in each. Reproduce one set of documents 20-23 for each group. Reproduce document 19 and worksheet F for each student.

a. Distribute document 19 and worksheet F to each student. Allow approximately 10-15 minutes for students to read the document and complete part A of the worksheet.

b. After students have completed part A of the worksheet, answer any questions they have about the document.

c. Consider what kinds of problems soldiers' families might have had to face with sons and husbands absent. How would the circumstances of black women differ from those of whites? Consider the plight of black families migrating North.

d. Form the class into groups. Give each group a set of documents 20-23. Direct each student to choose one letter. After reading the letter and completing part B of the worksheet, each student should share the contents of the letter with the group.

e. Discuss the evidence of hardships of blacks found within the documents. What conclusions does the evidence support?

5. Extended activities: The National Archives has two online resources for information about black soldiers in the Civil War. While researching one of the topics below, encourage your students to check these web sites:

"Preserving the Legacy of the United States Colored Troops" at **http://www.nara.gov/ education/teaching/usct/usctart.html** and "The Fight for Equal Rights: Black Soldiers in the Civil War at **http://www.nara.gov/education/teaching/usct/home.html**

a. Direct a small group of students to develop a time line that traces the changing roles of blacks in the American military from the American Revolution to the present.

b. Assign one or two students to research and report to the class the role of the United States Colored Troops in the Union war effort. The 54th Massachusetts Volunteer Infantry Regiment is the most well-documented of the black regiments.

c. Tell the students that during the Depression, the federal government instituted a project to record the experiences of black Americans who lived under slavery. These interviews were published in 1972 in a 19-volume set, *The American Slave: A Composite Autobiography*. Ask for volunteers to use some of these interviews to learn more about blacks during the Civil War and to evaluate another source of evidence for the class. As background, they may read C. Vann Woodward's critique of slave sources in "History from Slave Sources," *American Historical Review*, vol. 79, April 1974.

NOTE: For information on black soldiers in the Civil War, check these two web resources: "Preserving the Legacy of the United States Colored Troops" at **www.nara.gov/education/ teaching/usct/usctart** and "The Fight for Equal Rights: Black Soldiers in the Civil War" at **www.nara.gov/education/teaching**.

2

Exercise 2: Laborers, Contrabands, and Soldiers

Worksheet E

Directions: Use the information in document 11 to complete the worksheet.

Part A

1. Record factual information from the letter: writer(s), date written, to whom, from where, its subject.

2. List the men's grievances.

3. Is anyone singled out as being responsible for the injustices?

4. Quote lines that show:

    a. the men's willingness to work

    b. the men's sense of patriotism

5. Cite the line(s) that suggest corruption in the government.

6. What fears do the men express for their families?

7. What information is missing?

Part B

Write an argument based on information from the letter.

Exercise 2: Laborers, Contrabands, and Soldiers

Worksheet F

Directions: Use information in the documents and the time line to complete the worksheet.

Part A: Document 19

1. What kind of document is this? Who wrote it? To whom? When?

2. State the subject of the letter in one sentence.

3. Refer to the time line to see when black troops were first recruited. Comment on the timing of this document in relation to the federal policy of black recruitment.

4. In addition to banding together and writing this letter, what further steps have been taken by the men in the letter?

5. Can you find a line that expresses a sense of patriotism? If so, cite it.

6. Find the line that refers to black participation in an earlier war. Name the war.

7. Find a line that refers to families of blacks. Quote the line.

Part B: Documents 20-23

1. Who wrote the letter? To whom? When? Where was it written?

2. What are the chief concerns of the writer of the letter?

Exercise 3
The Battle of Ball's Bluff

Note to the Teacher:

As a part of Gen. George McClellan's defense of the Union capital of Washington, DC, a division under Gen. Charles Stone moved on the Confederates at Leesburg, VA, on October 21, 1861. The ensuing battle at Ball's Bluff, VA, was chosen for study in this unit because, although a small battle, its outcome was determined by many factors that are well documented. Most of this documentation was generated by an investigation conducted after the battle by the congressional Joint Committee on the Conduct of the War in its effort to appraise Union officers' competency in battle. These documents, used with the activities included in this exercise, give students the chance to look closely at a particular battle in the Civil War.

Initially students will study a map of the battle area and Union battle orders. Plotting Union and Confederate troop movements, students will follow the course of the battle. They will identify and weigh the causes of the Union defeat based on the documents reviewed. Next, they will analyze information from five officers' reports. Three of these reports were written by or from the point of view of Union officers. One was written by a Union officer who was not involved in the battle and, therefore, seems more objective. One was written by the commander of the Confederate forces at Ball's Bluff. Afterwards, students will synthesize the information learned by creating written or oral presentations.

Before beginning this exercise, refer students to the time line so that they gain a general understanding of events leading up to this battle. Use a map to locate the battle area. You may wish to refer students to the glossary to help them become familiar with military terminology.

Time: 1-5 class periods

Objectives:

- Describe the troop movements of the Union and Confederate armies during the Battle of Ball's Bluff, VA.

- Plot the events of the Battle of Ball's Bluff on a map.

- Evaluate the reasons for the defeat of the Union Army at the Battle of Ball's Bluff.

- Hypothesize about the impact of the Ball's Bluff battle on the course of the Civil War.

Materials Needed:

Documents 24-29
Worksheet G
Data Sheet
Glossary
Introduction Sheet
Sequence Sheets (Sunday and Monday)
Time line
Military Markers

Procedures:

1. **Day 1:** Divide the class into groups of three or four students each. Duplicate document 24 for each group and the introduction sheet for each student.

   a. As background for this activity, lead a class discussion in which you ask students to:

      1) Consider how a soldier might feel on the eve of his first battle.

      2) Describe what preparations might be made by soldiers and officers for an expected conflict.

      3) Speculate on how a volunteer soldier might feel about his life after 4 weeks of service with his company. If students have completed the exercise on Camp Life, encourage them to recall information discussed then.

   b. Divide the class into groups of three or four students each. Give each group a map. Encourage students to practice using the map by asking such questions as: What direction is Edward's Ferry from Leesburg? What direction is Harrison's Island from Conrad's Ferry? Identify the coordinates for Conrad's Ferry. What are the coordinates for the Copper Mine directly east of Leesburg?

   c. Tell the class that the following day they will return to these groups. Using the battle orders as interpreted by Union officers, they will retrace the battle that occurred at Ball's Bluff, VA.

   d. Assign the introduction sheet to students as homework. Remind them to bring it with them to class the next day.

2. **Day 2:** Regroup the students and provide each group with a copy of document 24 and one set of markers. Also provide each group with sequence sheets for Sunday and Monday, a copy of the Battle Orders, and a set of the students' instruction sheets.

   a. Instruct each group to appoint a group leader to read aloud the instruction sheet and a geographer to set up the map. Be sure all students are situated so they can see the map.

   b. Begin the battle exercise, directing students to follow the instructions provided.

   c. At the conclusion of the battle exercise, the group leaders should ask each student to list as many reasons as he or she can find for the defeat of the Union Army at Ball's Bluff, based on the information in the documents and the materials provided.

   d. When all groups have finished, conclude the exercise with a discussion focusing on these questions:

      1) Based on the documents and materials available to you, what were the reasons for the defeat of the Union Army at Ball's Bluff? Did any one reason, in your opinion, outweigh all others in importance? Cite statements from the materials to support your choice.

      2) What do you think was the critical point in the battle? Why?

3

    3) Which battle order do you judge to be the one that started the action? Why?

    4) Scholars, attempting to write a history of Ball's Bluff, draw conclusions as you have done from the sources available. What other records might a historian look for when writing an account of this battle?

3.   Reproduce for each student an introduction sheet (used in activity 1), worksheet G, and a data sheet. Assign the introduction sheet as homework.

    a.   Divide the class into five groups. Give each group a document from documents 25-29 and each student copies of worksheet G and the data sheet. Each group should read its letter and complete the worksheet.

    b.   After students have completed the worksheet, direct each group to select a spokesperson and ask him or her to present the group's interpretation of the battle, based on the group's document, to the class. Instruct students to record this information on their data sheets.

    c.   Lead a class discussion focusing on these questions: What is the bias of each writer? What are the possible causes of the bias of each? Which writer is most credible? Which is least credible? Why? Is it possible to affix blame for the Union defeat at Ball's Bluff? Why or why not?

    d.   Direct students to write their interpretations of the causes of the Union defeat at Ball's Bluff. Caution them to cite evidence from within the documents to support their arguments.

    e.   Upon completion of the written assignment, conduct a class discussion on bias to help extend students' understanding of the term beyond this exercise. Focus your discussion on such questions as the following: What is bias? What criteria should be used to judge the credibility of any source? Do these criteria also reflect bias? Why or why not?

While students should be able to draw some examples from the exercise, encourage them to cite other sources as well.

4.   In this exercise students write about some aspect of the Battle of Ball's Bluff using a literary or historical format. Allow several days for students to prepare their assignments. Make available the introduction sheet, sequence sheets, and battle orders. Students should bring their copies of the introduction to class.

    a.   Direct students to select one of these formats for their writing:

    1) A letter of a Union or Confederate soldier or officer written before or after the battle.

    2) An account of the battle written for a Southern or Northern newspaper.

    3) A poem evoking the emotional aspects of the battle.

    4) A diary entry for October 22, 1861.

    b.   Make available to students the sequence sheets and battle orders. Students should record specific data from these materials to use in their writing assignments.

MILITARY ACTION at BALL'S BLUFF ● October 21, 1861

71st PENN. RGT.	71st PENN. RGT.	71st PENN. RGT.	71st PENN. RGT.		Gorman's BRIG.	Gorman's BRIG.	Gorman's BRIG.	Gorman's BRIG.
1st MINN. RGT.	1st MINN. RGT.	1st MINN. RGT.	1st MINN. RGT.		15th MASS. RGT.	15th MASS. RGT.	15th MASS. RGT.	15th MASS. RGT.
15th SCOUT RGT.	15th SCOUT RGT.	15th SCOUT RGT.	15th SCOUT RGT.		19th MASS. RGT.	19th MASS. RGT.	19th MASS. RGT.	19th MASS. RGT.
20th MASS. RGT.	20th MASS. RGT.	20th MASS. RGT.	20th MASS. RGT.		42nd N.Y. RGT.	42nd N.Y. RGT.	42nd N.Y. RGT.	42nd N.Y. RGT.

UNION

CONFEDERATE

18th MISS. RGT.	18th MISS. RGT.	18th MISS. RGT.	18th MISS. RGT.		16th MISS. RGT.	16th MISS. RGT.	16th MISS. RGT.	16th MISS. RGT.
13th MISS. RGT.	13th MISS. RGT.	13th MISS. RGT.	13th MISS. RGT.		17th MISS. RGT.	17th MISS. RGT.	17th MISS. RGT.	17th MISS. RGT.
8th VA. RGT.	8th VA. RGT.	8th VA. RGT.	8th VA. RGT.		CAV.	CAV.	CAV.	CAV.
71st PENN.								

c. When the assignment is completed, ask students to share their work with their classmates in a format appropriate to your class.

d. As an alternative, some students may prefer to substitute an oral presentation for the writing assignment. You may wish to enlist the aid of a drama teacher for presentations such as the following:

1) Two veterans reminiscing about their experiences in battle.

2) A wounded soldier's monologue.

3) A mock trial of Charles P. Stone or George McClellan.

5. Extended activities: Ask students to research and report in writing or orally on one or several of these men connected with the Battle of Ball's Bluff.

a. Oliver Wendell Holmes, later an Associate Justice of the U.S. Supreme Court (1902-1932), was wounded at the battle as a member of the 20th Massachusetts Volunteers. Read his account of the battle.

b. Charles Stone's military career was affected because of this battle. Find out why he was imprisoned after the battle. What was Stone's connection with the Statue of Liberty in New York harbor?

c. Investigate how military commissions were given during the Civil War. What was Edward Baker's military background?

d. What kind of general was George McClellan? Find out about his relationship with President Lincoln. How did Gen. Robert E. Lee rate McClellan as an opponent?

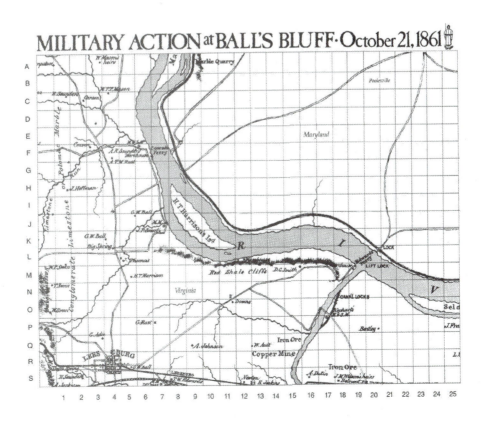

MILITARY ACTION at BALL'S BLUFF · October 21, 1861

Exercise 3: The Battle of Ball's Bluff

Worksheet G

Directions: Study your document carefully to answer the following questions.

1. Who wrote this report? To whom? Why?

2. According to this writer, what were the causes of the Union defeat at Ball's Bluff?

3. Does the writer think that good Confederate leadership or poor Union leadership caused the defeat? Other causes?

4. Is any one officer explicitly or implicitly blamed for the defeat? If so, who? Why?

Data Sheet

Use the spaces below to record information provided by each spokesperson about the actions of battle participants.

	1.	2.	3.	4.
Evans				
Stone				
Hinks				
Baker/Young				
McClellan				

Battle Orders

No. 1

RECEIVED OCTOBER 20, 1861, FROM CAMP GRIFFIN

THE GENERAL [MCCLELLAN] DESIRES THAT YOU KEEP A GOOD LOOKOUT UPON LEESBURG, TO SEE IF THIS MOVEMENT HAS THE EFFECT TO DRIVE THEM AWAY. PERHAPS A SLIGHT DEMONSTRATION ON YOUR PART WOULD HAVE THE EFFECT TO MOVE THEM.

A. V. COLBURN
Assistant Adjutant General

BRIGADIER GENERAL STONE, Poolesville

No. 2

HEADQUARTERS CORPS OF OBSERVATION
Poolesville, October 20, 1861

COLONEL:

YOU WILL PLEASE SEND ORDERS TO THE CANAL TO HAVE THE TWO NEW FLAT-BOATS NOW THERE OPPOSITE THE ISLAND [HARRISON'S] TRANSFERRED TO THE RIVER; AND WILL, AT THREE O'CLOCK p.m., HAVE THE ISLAND RE-ENFORCED BY ALL OF YOUR REGIMENT NOW ON DUTY AT THE CANAL AND AT THE NEW YORK BATTERY. THE PICKETS WILL BE REPLACED BY THE COMPANIES OF THE 19TH MASSACHUSETTS THERE.

VERY RESPECTFULLY,
YOUR OBEDIENT SERVANT,
CHA'S P. STONE
Brigadier General

COLONEL CHARLES DEVENS
Commanding 15th Regiment Massachusetts Volunteers

No. 3   (verbal order)

SEND CAPTAIN PHILBRICK OF YOUR REGIMENT WITH A SMALL PARTY ACROSS THE RIVER FROM HARRISON'S ISLAND AND HAVE HIM PUSH OUT WITHIN A MILE OF LEESBURG, IF POSSIBLE, WITHOUT BEING DISCOVERED. RETURN AND REPORT.

No. 4 (special order)

HEADQUARTERS CORPS OF OBSERVATION
Poolesville, October 20, 1861 — 10:30 p.m.

COLONEL DEVENS WILL LAND OPPOSITE HARRISON'S ISLAND WITH FIVE COMPANIES OF HIS REGIMENT, AND PROCEED TO SURPRISE THE CAMP OF THE ENEMY DISCOVERED BY CAPTAIN PHILBRICK, IN THE DIRECTION OF LEESBURG. THE LANDING AND MARCH WILL BE EFFECTED WITH SILENCE AND RAPIDITY.

COLONEL LEE, 20TH MASSACHUSETTS VOLUNTEERS, WILL IMMEDIATELY AFTER COLONEL DEVENS' DEPARTURE, OCCUPY HARRISON'S ISLAND WITH FOUR COMPANIES OF HIS REGIMENT, AND WILL CAUSE THE FOUR-OARED BOAT TO BE TAKEN ACROSS THE ISLAND TO THE POINT OF DEPARTURE OF COLONEL DEVENS. ONE COMPANY WILL BE THROWN ACROSS TO OCCUPY THE HEIGHTS ON THE VIRGINIA SHORE, AFTER COLONEL DEVENS'S DEPARTURE TO COVER HIS RETURN.

COLONEL DEVENS WILL ATTACK THE CAMP OF THE ENEMY AT DAYBREAK.

CHAS. P. STONE
Brigadier General

No. 5

HEADQUARTERS CORPS OF OBSERVATION
Edward's Ferry, October 20, 1861
10:50

COLONEL:

I AM INFORMED THAT THE FORCE OF THE ENEMY IS ABOUT 4,000 ALL TOLD. IF YOU CAN PUSH THEM YOU MAY DO SO, AS FAR AS TO HAVE A STRONG POSITION NEAR LEESBURG, IF YOU CAN KEEP THEM BEFORE YOU, AVOIDING THEIR BATTERIES.

REPORT FREQUENTLY, SO THAT WHEN THEY ARE PUSHED GORMAN CAN COME IN ON THEIR FLANK.

YOURS RESPECTFULLY
AND TRULY,
CHARLES P. STONE,
Brigadier General Commanding

COLONEL E. D. BAKER,
Commanding Brigade

3

No. 6

HEADQUARTERS CORPS OF OBSERVATION
Edward's Ferry, October 21, 1861

COLONEL:

IN CASE OF HEAVY FIRING IN FRONT OF HARRISON'S ISLAND YOU WILL ADVANCE
THE CALIFORNIA REGIMENT OF YOUR BRIGADE, OR RETIRE THE REGIMENTS UNDER
COLONELS LEE AND DEVENS NOW ON THE VIRGINIA SIDE OF THE RIVER, AT YOUR
DISCRETION, ASSUMING COMMAND ON YOUR ARRIVAL.

VERY RESPECTFULLY,
COLONEL, YOUR
MOST OBEDIENT SERVANT,

CHARLES P. STONE
Brigadier General Commanding
COLONEL E. D. BAKER

Exercise 3: The Battle of Ball's Bluff

Introduction Sheet*

BULLETIN:
Several Regiments Stone's Command
Driven from Virginia Opposite Harrison's Island.
General Edward Baker Dead.

October 21, 1861, was, as one observer remembered it later, "a lovely, a rare October day." It was a day that was to be a personal tragedy for a handful of men and one that would have grave consequences for the Union cause. On that day, a few regiments of Gen. George B. McClellan's Army of the Potomac were led into ambush on high bluffs overlooking the Potomac River. The men were routed from the bluffs and scrambled to the edge of the river. Confederate infantrymen, commanded by Gen. N. G. Evans, charged to the top of the cliffs. Even in the failing light of dusk, the Northern soldiers were easy targets, trapped at the edge of the river. Enemy fire poured down on the Yankees. A young first lieutenant, Oliver Wendell Holmes, later a justice of the U.S. Supreme Court, was gravely wounded and lay near death. Paul Revere, grandson of the Revolutionary War hero, was reported missing. Hundreds of men were taken prisoner; dozens were killed. Among the dead was Gen. Edward Baker, a powerful politician, a former U.S. Senator, and a close personal friend of Abraham Lincoln.

President Lincoln was at the Headquarters of the Army of the Potomac when news of the disaster was relayed. A newspaper correspondent present recalled, "Five minutes passed and then Mr. Lincoln, his breast heaving, passed through the room. He almost fell as he passed into the street...but he did not fall."

Reaction throughout the North to this action, called the Battle of Ball's Bluff, was first shock and then a deep bitterness. The Union armies were not faring well in these early days of the Civil War. This new disaster pushed many people close to the limit of their patience with, and faith in, the federal army. Baker's friends directed vague accusations of treason, or at least incompetence, at his superiors. Powerful political pressure was exerted to have Maj. Gen. Charles Stone, long a trusted officer in the U.S. Army, relieved of his command and tried as a traitor. Newspapers printed sensational, often spurious accounts of the battle. To heighten the confusion, the army suppressed some reports of the action.

What had happened at Ball's Bluff? Historians seeking to answer that question have relied on primary documents: the actual battle orders sent and received by the officers involved, official accounts of the battle written by soldiers in its aftermath, as well as maps and other guides on which troop movements could be plotted and terrain features studied.

Many of these documents survive in the National Archives. Some have been reproduced in this package. In the following exercises you will be asked to use these sources of information, seeking to answer such questions as: How was the battle fought? What factors weighed in its outcome? Can blame for the defeat be fixed?

---

* This introduction sheet was written by members of the National Archives education staff, using available sources.

Exercise 3: The Battle of Ball's Bluff

Sequence Sheets*

Sunday, October 20, 1861

Morning: *General McClellan telegraphs General Stone at Poolesville (order 1).*

Afternoon: Stone moves Gorman's Brigade to Edward's Ferry and crosses the 1st Minnesota to the Virginia side.
[Gorman's Brigade to K-21, K-22]   [1st Minn. to N-20]

1 p.m.:   *Stone sends communication to Colonel Devens (order 2).*

Dusk: *Stone sends verbal order to Devens (order 3).*

Evening: Captain Philbrick crosses the Potomac River with 15-20 men, proceeds to reconnoiter towards Leesburg.
[15th Scout to N-6]

Evening: Philbrick pushes out toward Leesburg, VA. In the failing light he sights what appears to be a small enemy camp. This is reported to Stone.
[15th Scout to O-6]

10:30 p.m.:   *Stone sends special orders to Devens (order 4).*
[15th Mass. to N-6] [20th Mass. to J-9]

Evening: Stone sends order to Baker (order 5).

Midnight: Stone orders Colonel Baker to send the California Regiment (71st Penn.) to Conrad's Ferry and to wait there for further orders.

Monday, October 21, 1861

Dawn: Devens crosses the river at dawn and climbs the 70-foot bluffs that have blocked the Union view of the Virginia side of the river. He searches for the enemy camp reported by Philbrick. He discovers Philbrick's men had mistaken a row of trees for an enemy camp in the failing light of the previous evening. Devens advances with his force to within a mile of Leesburg, examines the countryside, and posts his troops in the woods to await further orders.
[15th Mass., 15th Scout to P-8]

7 a.m.:   Rebel riflemen appear from the direction of Conrad's Ferry. Confederate cavalry approach from Leesburg. Devens holds his ground.
[18th Miss. to P-5, Q-5]

| **8 a.m.:** | *Stone sends second communication to Baker (order 6).* |

8–9 a.m.: Stone tells Devens he is to be supported; General Baker is to arrive with reinforcements and take command. Devens' men are hard pressed by the oncoming Confederates. He sends a scout to the river to check on Baker's troops.

Noon: Attacks on Devens' command increase. (Some of his men are using the inaccurate Belgian musket against the better-armed, on-coming Confederate troops.) Receiving no orders and seeing no reinforcements, Devens starts to fall back to the river.
[15th Mass., 15th Scout to M-6] [Cav. to N-6]
[16th Miss. to M-5, N-5]

71st Penn.

Baker has arrived on Harrison's Island. He spends most of the morning struggling to get a few cannons across the river. Baker now considers whether to recall troops from the Virginia side of the river or to reinforce them. Cries are heard from the bluffs calling for assistance. Baker begins to send the California (71st Penn.) and Tammany (42d N.Y.) regiments across the river. He has three flatboats, two small skiffs, and a metallic lifeboat to put hundreds of men across the swift river.
[71st Penn. to J-7]   [42d N.Y. to K-7]

1–2 p.m.: Baker joins Devens and assumes command. The force includes the 15th Mass., 20th Mass., 19th Mass., the Tammany regiment, and the California regiment.
[20th Mass. to L-8]   [19th Mass. to M-9l

2–3 p.m.: Confederate attack continues on the Union right, moves to center and left where it grows in intensity.
[8th Va. to J-6]   [17th Miss. to K-6, L-6]

4–5 p.m.: Battle continues. Baker is killed. The Union line wavers and begins to come apart. Col. Milton Cogswell assumes command and tries to cut through to Gorman's Brigade at Edward's Ferry.
[19th Mass. to M-11] [15th Mass., 15th Scout on M-10]

Mississippi regiments arrive to cut off Cogswell's retreat. Union line dissolves and troops flee down the bluffs toward the river.
[13th Miss. to N-10, N-11, M-12, M-13]

Dusk: Confederate fire pours from the top of the cliffs. Sharpshooters riddle the overloaded Union boats, forcing many soldiers to swim unprotected from the enemy fire. With the failing light, many of the swimming soldiers become confused in their attempt to reach the Maryland side of the river. A few manage to return to the Union lines; the greater number are killed or captured.

* These sequence sheets were written by members of the National Archives education staff, using available sources. Material in italics is taken from the actual battle orders.

3

Exercise 3: The Battle of Ball's Bluff

Students' Instruction Sheet

For the Group Leader

1. Ask the geographer to place troops in their starting locations.

2. Put the six battle orders in a pile, arranging them so that order No. 1 is on top. Place these in the center of the group next to the map. (Battle orders are indicated on the sequence sheet in italicized type.)

3. Give the sequence sheet for Sunday to one member of your group. Give Monday's sequence sheet to another group member. These students will read aloud from these sheets.

4. Tell the group that they will trace the battle through Union battle orders and interpret them just as the Union commanders did. Begin the battle by directing the student holding the sequence sheet for Sunday to announce the time of day (Morning) and the information that corresponds to it. The italicized type indicates that battle order No. 1 should be drawn next by another member of the group and read aloud. The student holding the Sunday sequence sheet will continue to read through the events for that day, announcing the time of day and the accompanying information. When troop names and coordinates are indicated within the brackets, the geographer should move troops to their new locations. Pause to allow time for these changes. Continue reading aloud until the battle ends, at dusk on Monday, October 21, 1861.

5. List the factors, as the group sees them, that determined the Union defeat at Ball's Bluff, VA.

For the Geographer

1. Place Union troops at these starting locations:

   Gen. Stone's headquarters (HQ) is at Poolesville, at coordinate A-20.

   Gorman's Brigade, including the 1st Minn., is on the road to Edward's Ferry, squares G-20, 21 and 22.

   Devens' Regiment, the 15th Mass., is on the Maryland side of the river, H-10.

   Philbrick's scout detachment (15th Scout) is located on Harrison's Island, J-9.

   The Tammany Regiment (42d N.Y.), the California Regiment (71st Penn.) and Cogswell's 19th Mass. are at Conrad's Ferry; E-8, D-9, C-9, respectively.

   The 20th Mass., under Colonel Lee, is on the Maryland side of the Potomac River at H-11.

2. Place the Confederate regiments at these locations:

   North of Leesburg:
   (2 markers) 18th Miss. at P-2, P-3
   (2 markers) 17th Miss. at L-2, L-3
   8th Va. at J-3
   Jennifer's cavalry (Cav.) at Q-6

   West of Edward's Ferry:
   (4 markers) 13th Miss. at O-11, P-12, Q-13, and R-14.

3. As the battle progresses, troop movements occur. These are indicated by bracketed coordinates on the sequence sheets, and they will be announced to you by students reading those sheets. Move the markers according to the instructions within the brackets. Example: [20th Mass. to J-10.]

Exercise 4
War and Technology

Note to the Teacher:

It is a cliche of history that war advances technological development. The central question the student is asked to consider here is whether this generalization can be tested. Does war advance technological development? Impede it? What technology is advanced and what is impeded? What evidence is available? The documents in this exercise illustrate various aspects of these questions and introduce students to the process of comparing and weighing conflicting evidence.

Before beginning this exercise, conduct a general class discussion on the state of technology in the pre-Civil War era. Touch on the state of industry and agriculture and the nature of warfare in the 19th century.

Time: 1-3 class periods

Objectives:

* Use a graph to chart the growth or stagnation of specific industries during the Civil War.

* Discuss several ways in which wartime technology affected late 19th-century society.

* Describe the changes in medical/surgical procedures within the military during the Civil War.

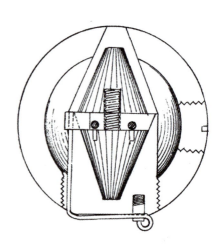

Materials Needed:

Documents 30-42
Worksheets H-K
Time line
Bibliography

Procedures:

1. Duplicate one set of documents 30-33 and copies of worksheet H for each student. Divide the class into 3 groups.

    a. Distribute document 30 to one group, documents 31 and 32 to one group, and document 33 to the other group. Provide each student with a worksheet.

    b. Direct students to discuss the questions on the worksheet and record their answers. When a group has finished working with a document(s), they should pass it along to another group so that all questions on the worksheet can be completed.

    c. Discuss the questions on the worksheet with the class. Using the evidence given here, assess the effects of changing technology on warfare during the Civil War.

2. Reproduce documents 34 and 35 and worksheet I for each student.

   a. Distribute the documents and worksheets to students and direct students to complete the worksheet.

   b. Discuss how the Civil War affected the animal trap, artificial leg, and armor-plating industries. Also consider what other industries might have been affected by the war.

   c. How do these technological changes compare with those of World War I, World War II, and Vietnam?

3. Divide the class into 4 groups. Reproduce two sets of documents 36-40 for each group and copies of worksheet J for each student.

   a. Distribute two sets of documents 36-40 to each group and copies of worksheet J to each student.

   b. Instruct students to share the documents within the group to allow each student to complete the worksheet questions. To help in this process, half of the group might complete part 2 of the worksheet, while the other half completes part 1. Note that documents 39 and 40 are longer than the other documents used in this exercise. You may wish to assign those documents to the faster readers in each group and ask them to share the information from those documents with the rest of the group members. Allow the groups adequate time to complete the worksheet.

   c. Discuss with the class the relationship between war and medical technology. Focus your discussion on the questions: Does war seem to impede or advance medical technology? Why?

4. Post documents 30, 41, and 42 at a place accessible to all students. Reproduce worksheet K for each student.

   a. Discuss the purpose of patents with students as a group.

   b. Allow students time to look carefully at each document and complete the worksheet.

   c. Discuss question 2 on the worksheet with students. Consider which of the three inventions has had the greatest impact on warfare since the Civil War.

5. Extended activities: Ask students to choose a long-term project from the following suggestions.

   a. Research the technological changes caused by different wars. Some examples are: nuclear energy, agricultural changes, anesthetics, and convenience foods like instant coffee.

   b. Develop a list of the technological changes stimulated by the Civil War, World War I, World War II, and Vietnam.

   c. "The role of war in promoting industrial progress had been small compared with the role of industrial progress in bringing on war" (John Nef, *War and Human Progress*). Research this statement in terms of the Civil War.

   d. Consider how nuclear weapons have altered the nature of warfare. Compare and contrast these changes with changes in the Civil War era.

Exercise 4: War and Technology

Worksheet H

Directions: Read documents 30-33 carefully to answer the following questions.

Document 30: In the Civil War, battles were waged as general mass movements of troops against an enemy position. Rifle fire was used to break an attack or chase defenders from an area.

1. Write a description of the weapon depicted in the patent drawing, citing the important elements in its design.

2. Do you think the machine gun is an offensive or defensive weapon? Explain your answer.

3. How do you think this weapon would affect the tactics of warfare as described above?

Documents 31 and 32

1. Does the examiner favor this device? Why or why not?

2. Considering the nature of combat in the Civil War, how might this new weapon alter warfare?

Document 33: Note the date of the experiment and refer to the time line to gauge the state of affairs in the north at the time of this experiment. One historian, in describing this incident, said it was a "miracle" Lincoln and his cabinet members were not killed or seriously injured in the rocket explosion. Considering these circumstances, why do you think the President was asked to personally view this dangerous experiment?

Exercise 4: War and Technology

Worksheet I

Directions: Study documents 34 and 35 to complete the worksheet.

1. Note the list of animal trap inventions in document 34. Throughout most of the years in the middle decades of the 1800's, fur trapping and making garments from furs was a big business in the United States.

   a. The Civil War started in April 1861 and ended 4 years later, in April 1865. Using the dates in the right column of this document, calculate how many patents for animal trap inventions were filed in the 4 years before the war (April 1857–March 1861), during the war years, and the 4 years following the war (April 1865–March 1869).

   b. Plot a line graph of your findings.

   c. According to your graph, what effect did war have on the technology of animal trapping?

   d. What might be some of the reasons for this effect?

   e. Do you think this effect would extend to other industries? Why or why not?

2. Refer to document 35. Note the list of artificial arm inventions.

   a. Using the dates suggested in question 1.a., determine the number of a patents filed before, during, and after the war.

   b. Plot a graph of your findings.

   c. Compare your two graphs.

   d. What deductions can you make about technology during the Civil War and the relationship between war and technology?

3. Note in document 35 the listings for armor-plating.

   a. Consulting the time line, what event might have accounted for the heavy cluster of patents filed from mid-1862 to early 1863.

   b. How is this example different from the previous two? Why?

Exercise 4: War and Technology

Worksheet J

Directions: Read document 36 to answer questions 1-3 and documents 37-40 to answer questions 4-7.

1. Who is the writer of this report?

2. How might his opinion be biased? Why?

3. What accounts for the mass changes to which the writer refers?

4. What might have been the surgeons' purpose in writing documents 37 and 38?

5. How might soldiers have benefited from these letters?

6. What do these letters tell you about the state of surgical arts in the 1860's?

7. Do these letters seem to support or contradict the statements made in document 36? Explain.

Exercise 4: War and Technology

Worksheet K

Directions: Study documents 30, 41, and 42 to complete this worksheet.

1. Answer the following questions for each patent:

   a. When was the patent filed?

   b. Who was the inventor?

   c. Where did the inventor live?

   d. Briefly describe the invention to be patented.

2. Which invention do you think would have the greatest effect on warfare? List at least three reasons for your answer.

Exercise 5
Civilians and Government

Note to the Teacher:

More than 100 years after the American Civil War, certain images of that war remain vivid in the American consciousness: Pickett's brigades massing for the doomed charge at Gettysburg; rumpled, cigar-smoking Ulysses S. Grant planning the strategies to finally wear down the army of General Lee; the army of Stonewall Jackson blazing up the Shenandoah Valley, throwing Washington, DC, into a state of panic.

Beyond the battles and leaders there was another war in the 1860s. Not nearly as glorious as the others, it is discussed or remembered much less often. But it was closer to what a civil war really is; that is, citizens in conflict with their government, their families, and their neighbors.

The principal objective of this exercise is to develop students' skills in using primary sources while they learn how a civil war affects the lives of citizens and the workings of government. Students should be reminded that their conclusions are based on limited evidence and are, therefore, tentative.

In the following exercises, students read and analyze documents that indicate that the rights of private citizens are less secure in times of internal turmoil. First, they review evidence of military authority superceding civil authority and the consequences. After introducing a decree issued in 1863 by President Abraham Lincoln formally suspended the writ of habeas corpus, your students will examine the ways in which the decree altered citizens' lives.

While studying the conflict between civil and military interests during the Civil War, students will make some basic judgments about the ethics of these occurrences. Using evidence from the documents, students play the role of a military court and render a verdict in a mock trial. They become aware of the need to balance an individual's rights and national security. Students weigh both sides of this issue and develop their own conclusions.

Finally students will review another aspect of the civil war, that of conflict within families and between neighbors. Through a role-playing exercise students will consider the effects of a civil war on one family shattered by the conflict. They weigh the motives of these individuals and discuss the ethics of their actions.

Time: 1-5 class periods

Objectives:

- Identify some of the personal concerns of civilians caught in the social turmoil of the Civil War.

- Examine the courses of action taken by members of a family during the Civil War and state the values implicit in those actions.

- List several ways in which the Civil War affected civil rights and personal liberties.

- Evaluate the effects of the suspension of writs of habeas corpus by President Lincoln.

Materials Needed:

Documents 43-54
Worksheets L-N
Copies of the Bill of Rights

Procedures:

To complete some of these activities, students need a working knowledge of the Bill of Rights and the application of the writ of habeas corpus. Make copies of the Bill of Rights available to students. Before using these materials, conduct a class discussion about them and about the nature of a civil war.

1. Divide the class into three groups. Make a set of documents 43-45 for each group and reproduce worksheet L for each student. Post document 46 in a place accessible to all students, and make certain all students have access to a copy of the Bill of Rights.

   a. Distribute copies of the documents and the worksheet.

   b. Direct each group to discuss the questions on the worksheet and have group members record their answers individually.

   c. Conclude this exercise with a discussion of the rights of an individual and the pressures on a government engaged in a war. Consider under what circumstances the government should curtail individual rights.

2. Divide the class into four groups. Reproduce one set of documents 45, 47, and 48 for each group. (If you have completed exercise 1, you will have 3 copies of document 45.) Duplicate worksheet M for each student.

   a. Conduct a class discussion about the writ of habeas corpus. Discuss also the peculiar relationship between the border states and the federal government during the Civil War.

   b. Distribute copies of the documents and worksheet.

   c. When the worksheets are complete, discuss with students what conclusions they have drawn from the documents. Consider such questions as: Why do you think Lincoln issued this decree? Do you think his action was justified? On what grounds?

3. Reproduce 4 sets of documents 43, 46, and 54. Divide the class into two groups and give each group two copies of each document.

   a. Assign one group to "defend" H. Lick and the other group to "prosecute" him.

   b. Provide time for the groups to prepare their "cases" using the evidence in the documents.

   c. Ask each group to share with the class the evidence from the documents that seems to support Lick's guilt or innocence.

5

d. At the close of the group presentations, direct students to discuss the guilt or innocence of Lick. Consider whether their opinions might change in peacetime.

4. Reproduce 4 sets of documents 49-51. Divide the class into two groups and give each group two copies of each document. You may wish to use this exercise with activity 3 for the purpose of comparing the two cases.

   a. Assign one group to "defend" Joseph Hedges and the other group to "prosecute" him.

   b. Provide time for the groups to prepare their "cases" using the evidence in the documents.

   c. Ask each group to share with the class the evidence from the documents that seems to support Hedges' guilt or innocence.

   d. At the close of the group presentations, ask students to discuss the guilt or innocence of Hedges. Ask them to consider whether their opinions might change in peacetime.

5. Divide the class into 3 groups. Reproduce documents 50, 52, and 53 for each group. Reproduce worksheet N for each student.

   a. Distribute the documents and worksheets.

   b. Instruct the groups to discuss the answers to the worksheet questions and record their responses individually.

   c. Use question 4 on the worksheet as the basis for a discussion of how people respond to a civil war. How do the characters in the documents justify their actions? How would you act in similar situations?

6. Extended activities

   a. Possible discussion or student research topics include:
      1) Conscription
      2) Rationing of essential goods
      3) Profiteering
      4) Freedom of speech/publication limitations
      5) Rights of resident aliens during wartime
      6) Role of national security

   b. During the Civil War, the federal government instituted a policy of conscription to raise an army. Discuss with students the pro's and con's of such a policy. Consider where individual rights fit in such a system.

   c. Discuss with students what limitations on individual liberty a government should enforce during wartime.

Exercise 5: Civilians and Government

Worksheet L

1. Answer as many of the following questions as possible using documents 43-45:

   a. Who wrote the letter? To whom was it written?

   b. When was the letter written?

   c. Where was the letter written?

   d. What is the subject of the letter?

2. Refer to the Bill of Rights. Do these letters offer evidence of support or violation of those rights? Why?

3. Read document 46, column 2, "General Rosecrans on Freedom of the Press." What is General Rosecrans' position? Do you agree or disagree with him? Why?

4. Read document 46, column 1. How do you think Rosecrans would respond to this article?

Exercise 5: Civilians and Government

Worksheet M

1. Examine document 47.

    a. What is the subject of this document?

    b. Who wrote it?

    c. When does it take effect?

2. Read document 48.

    a. Where is the writer located? Is this location significant?

    b. When was the letter written?

    c. What is the subject of the letter?

3. What is the connection between the two documents? How might the letter writer's situation have been different if the proclamation had not been issued?

4. Read document 45.

    a. When was it written?

    b. Why is the date significant?

    c. What does it tell you about conditions in the country before document 47 was issued?

Exercise 5: Civilians and Government

Worksheet N

1. Examine document 52.

    a. Write a brief description of this document.

    b. Imagine that you are a citizen of Missouri in the early days of the Civil War with no clear ideas about what is happening. How would you feel about being asked to sign this document?

2. Read document 53.

    a. List evidence of the writer's bias.

    b. What does the writer indicate is the motive for this letter?

    c. What other possible motives can you imagine?

3. Read document 50.

    a. To whom is the letter directed?

    b. What is it about?

    c. List the names of the brothers mentioned in the letter.

    d. What is the current status of each brother?

4. Document 50 was written in late 1864, just a few months before the end of the Civil War. Imagine a Hedges' family gathering after the war. Take the role of one of the members of the family.

    a. Joseph, the military prisoner.

    b. John, the Confederate guerrilla.

    c. Briscoe, the Union soldier.

    d. Fanny, their sister

Based on evidence in the letter, outline why you chose your course of action during the war.

Time Line

Nov. 6, 1860	Abraham Lincoln is elected President.
Dec. 20, 1860	South Carolina secedes from the Union.
Apr. 12, 1861	Fort Sumter is fired upon.
Apr. 15. 1861	Lincoln calls for 75,000 troops to suppress the rebellion.
Spring 1861	Virginia, Tennessee, North Carolina, and Arkansas secede from the Union, giving the Confederacy its final states. Alabama, Arkansas, Florida, Georgia, Louisiana, Mississippi, North Carolina, South Carolina, Tennessee, Texas, and Virginia now belong to the Confederate States of America. This grouping will remain constant until the war's end.
July 21, 1861	Battle of Bull Run. Northerners are stunned by this rout of the Union Army by Confederate forces. Hopes for a lightning conclusion to the war begin to fade in both North and South.
Oct. 21, 1861	Northern hopes sink lower as a result of the Battle of Ball's Bluff. The battle, although small in scale, seems to confirm the supremacy of the Confederate Army and the futility of the Union war effort.
Dec. 1861	The "Trent Affair." Confederate emissaries James Mason and John Slidell, bound for Europe on a British ship, are captured by officers of the U. S. Navy. Outraged, the English demand their release. For a while, war with both England and France appears imminent. After complicated negotiations and political maneuverings, Lincoln releases the two prisoners.
Spring 1862	A series of Union victories in the Western theatre; the taking of Forts Henry and Donelson, on the Tennessee and Cumberland rivers, respectively; the defeat of a Confederate force at Mill Springs, KY; and the apparent strength of the Eastern Army of the Potomac under new commander George McClellan renew Northern hopes of a victory by the end of 1862.
Mar. 9, 1862	Two odd, ironclad warships of a type never before engaged in combat, the U.S.S. *Monitor* and the C.S.S. *Virginia* (also known as the *Merrimac*), meet at Hampton Roads, VA. Although the fight is inconclusive, the nature of naval warfare here after changes.
Apr. 6 & 7,1862	The fierce, bloody battle of Shiloh produces the largest casualty lists of the war so far. Northerners and Southerners both have a renewed sense of the horrors of civil war.
May 1862	The Confederate Army of Shenandoah, under Thomas "Stonewall" Jackson sweeps through northwestern Virginia, threatening to capture the Union government at Washington, DC. Many Southerners feel the pendulum of the war has again, perhaps finally, swung to their side.
June 26- July 2, 1862	McClellan's Army of the Potomac is forced to abandon its campaign on Richmond by vigorous attacks from the Army of Northern Virginia under Robert E. Lee.
Aug. 29, 1862	The Confederate forces of Lee and Jackson combine to inflict a demoralizing defeat on Union forces at the old Bull Run battlefield. Washington is again temporarily panicked. A sense of gloom settles on many Northerners as a result of the setbacks.

Sept.-Oct. 1862	Buoyed by the victories of their armies, Confederate commanders launch twin offensives into Maryland in the east and Kentucky in the west. Southern morale is high. Southerners sense that victories on Union soil will lead England and France to recognize the Confederacy as a sovereign nation and offer foreign aid, almost certainly assuring Southern independence. These Confederate drives are halted at the battles of Antietam in Maryland and Perryville in Kentucky. Although inconclusive from a military point of view, these battles, especially Antietam, have a far-reaching impact.
Sept. 22, 1862	Seizing the opportunity afforded by the victory at Antietam, Lincoln issues the preliminary Emancipation Proclamation declaring slaves in the states of rebellion "then thence forward and forever free" as of January 1, 1863. Although freeing only the slaves in the territory in rebellion, this proclamation for the first time firmly and unmistakably links the Union war effort with the abolition of slavery. As an added benefit, it swings European public sentiment to the Northern side of the Civil War, dimming chances of recognition of the Confederacy.
Sept. 1862	Abraham Lincoln suspends writs of habeas corpus. Throughout the conflict, especially in border areas such as Kentucky and Missouri, the true meaning of the Civil War has been manifested by wholesale imprisonings of those deemed disloyal. Lincoln's suspension of habeas corpus affirms the supremacy, at least for the period of the war, of military over civil authority.
Dec. 1862	The second year of war ends dismally for the North with a disastrous beating in the east at Fredericksburg, VA, and a vicious, unrewarding fight at Murfreesboro, TN, in the west. On the surface the Confederacy seems as strong as ever; in the east, Union armies have been consistently whipped and kept from the Southern capital at Richmond. In the west, the South still holds most of Tennessee, all of the deep South, and the vital stretch of the Mississippi between northern Mississippi and southern Louisiana. But another reality is emerging. The South is beginning to suffer from shortages of practically everything necessary to wage war: food, clothing, new weaponry, and industrial technology.
Jan. 1, 1863	The Emancipation Proclamation takes effect. Lincoln authorizes the enrollment of freed slaves in the army and the navy.
Spring 1863	Eager to win a decisive victory in the east, the Union Army, under Joseph Hooker, once again pushes "onward to Richmond." In early May, through the brilliant generalship of Lee and Jackson, the Union army is shattered at Chancellorsville, VA. Southerners celebrate the victory, but mourn the loss of "Stonewall" Jackson, killed in the battle. Lee now leads the Confederate Army into the Union state of Pennsylvania. This is partly a response to the victory at Chancellorsville. More importantly, Lee seeks to replenish badly exhausted Confederate supplies of food and clothing and defeat the Union Army on Northern soil. This is seen as the last chance to induce European nations to lend economic aid that the South now desperately needs.
July 1-4, 1863	Lee's army suffers a decisive defeat at the Battle of Gettysburg during the first 3 days of July. The Confederates retreat to Virginia, having mounted the last large scale invasion of the North in the war. Of even greater strategic importance, U. S. Grant's western army captures Vicksburg. This action, and the later capture of Port Hudson, LA, opens the Mississippi River to Northern commerce and splits the Confederacy in two.
Spring 1864	Gen. Ulysses S. Grant is appointed head of the entire Union Army. He places William T. Sherman in charge of the armies in the west. Sherman sets off on his bloody and destructive march, first to the city of Atlanta, then to the sea. Grant commences his grim campaign to grind down Lee's army in Virginia.

Summer 1864	In the east and west, Union and Confederate forces are engaged in almost constant contact. Although from a military standpoint the North is clearly winning the war, this is not always apparent to civilians. What is clear and readily understood is the size of the casualty lists issuing from small towns in Georgia and Virginia. The war has now raged unabated for 3 years. Many, in both the North and the South, are sick of the war and are ready to seek whatever means necessary to bring it to a close. The year 1864 is an election year; Lincoln himself despairs of being re-elected.
Nov. 8, 1864	By election day, Lee's army is under siege south of Richmond at Petersburg. Sherman has taken Atlanta and appears certain to march through the Carolinas. Cheered by these events, Northerners re-elect Lincoln by a resounding majority. The South's last chance, a political change in the North, vanishes.
Dec. 21, 1864	Sherman captures the city of Savannah, GA, completing his march to the sea.
Dec. 22, 1864	Lee's weary, starving army is driven from Petersburg. Lee moves westward in a desperate effort to join forces with other Confederate armies. His retreat is cut off near the small crossroads of Appomattox Court House, VA.
Apr. 9, 1865	Lee surrenders his army. General Joseph Johnston later surrenders the last large Confederate army to Sherman in North Carolina. The Civil War ends.
Apr. 14, 1865	Lincoln is assassinated.

Glossary

Adjutant General	The chief administrative officer of the U. S. Army.
affidavit	A written declaration made under oath before a notary public or other authorized official.
aide-de-camp	A military officer acting as secretary and confidential assistant to a senior officer.
artillery	The branch of an armed force that specializes in the use of large, mounted guns.
battalion	A regiment or any part of a regiment composed of two or more companies.
battery	A tactical artillery unit corresponding to the level of a "company" in the infantry.
bounty	A payment given by a government for enlisting in the military service.
brigade	A unit of the U.S. Army composed of two or more regiments.
Butler, Benjamin Franklin	Union general (1818-93) who in May 1861 was appointed major general of volunteers. He became military governor of New Orleans in May 1862, when the city surrendered. Given command of the Department of Eastern Virginia, he allowed his army to be caught at Bermuda Hundred, VA, by a smaller Confederate force.
Cavalry	Troops trained to fight on horseback.
conscript	One who is drafted into the armed forces.
contraband	An escaped slave who fled to or was taken behind Union lines.
detachment	The dispatch of troops from a larger unit for a special duty or mission.
double quick	A marching pace of 180 three-foot steps per minute.
enfranchisement	To free; to endow with the rights of citizenship, especially the right to vote.
entrenchment	A fortification; a series of banked trenches.
fatigue duty	Manual labor, such as "cutting roads," assigned to soldiers.
guerrilla	A member of a small, independent band of soldiers that harasses the enemy by surprise raids.
impress	To force into military service.
infantry	The branch of an army made up of units trained to fight on foot.
inst.	Instant; used in letters to mean the present or current month.
militia	A civilian army, as distinct from a body of professional soldiers.
musket	A heavy large-caliber gun for infantry soldiers; predecessor of the modern rifle.
muster (in, out)	To enlist someone in or discharge someone from military service.
oath of allegiance	A formal declaration of loyalty to a country.
ordinance	An authoritative command or order enacted by a city or government.
ordnance	A branch of the U.S. Army that designs, develops, stores, maintains, and issues weapons.
picket	One or more soldiers advanced or held in readiness to give warning of an enemy approach.
Provost Marshal	The head of the military police.
reconnaissance	A survey made of a region to examine its terrain to determine the tactical placement of military forces.

reconnoiter	To make a preliminary inspection of an enemy's position and strength.
regiment	Ten companies of infantry.
retaliation	To return like for like, as in a "retaliatory" attack.
rout	A disorderly retreat following defeat; an overwhelming defeat.
secesh	Nickname for a U.S. secessionist.
Stanton, Edwin M.	Union Secretary of War, 1862-68.
Surgeon General	The chief of medical services in one of the armed services.
sutler	A merchant who followed an army and sold provisions to the soldiers.
ult.	Ultimo; used in letters to mean in or of the preceding month.
United States Christian Commission	An organization founded to minister to the religious needs of soldiers; distributed writing paper and other supplies to them;and received and answered inquiries about them.
vols.	Volunteers
writ of habeas corpus	A formal order issued by a court requiring that a person be brought before a judge or court, especially for investigation of a restraint of that person's liberty. It is used as a protection against illegal imprisonment.
your obt. servt.	Your obedient servant; a popular closing for a letter during the Civil War era.

Annotated Bibliography

The following books either contribute specifically to understanding the topics included in this package or serve as a general background for enhancing study of the Civil War.

Books listed include accounts published in the immediate post-war era as well as more contemporary works. Some of the titles are more suitable for teachers, others make good reading for high school students. We have suggested in each annotation what we feel to be the appropriate audience for each book.

The list is not meant to be definitive. We have chosen these works from the hundreds of volumes published on various aspects of the war. We feel that some of these will enhance study of the topics in this package and of the Civil War-period in general.

General Interest

American Heritage Picture History of the Civil War. New York: American Heritage Publishing Co., Inc., 1960.

> More than 600 pages, this book is a lavishly illustrated, colorful, and succinctly written panorama of the Civil War. Recommended as an introduction to those learning about the war.

Catton, Bruce. *The Coming Fury*. New York: Doubleday & Company, Inc., 1961.

_____. *Terrible Swift Sword*. New York: Doubleday & Company, Inc., 1963.

_____. *Never Call Retreat*. New York: Doubleday & Company, Inc., 1965.

> This three-volume set was written as a centennial history of the Civil War. Catton deftly interweaves military, political, and social themes. Perhaps no other writer so successfully conveys to lay readers the epic quality of the American Civil War. Catton is equally dexterous dealing with the upper echelons of the Lincoln and Davis administrations, the black experience during the war, military campaigns, and other themes. Recommended for students and teachers.

Freeman, Douglas Southall. *Lee's Lieutenants*. New York: Scribner, 1998.

> This is a classic three-volume set on the command structure of the Confederate Army of Northern Virginia. Scrupulously researched, the work is written with dramatic flair. These books embody much of the romantic vision of "the lost cause" and warfare during the 1860's. Suggested for students.

Heidler, David S. and Jeanne T. Heidler. *Encyclopedia of the American Civil War*. Santa Barbara, CA: ABC-CLIO, 2000.

> A five-volume reference work, this set covers almost every aspect of the Civil War in great detail and includes maps and photographs as well as a general chronology of events. All entries were written by established scholars who present material in a clear and concise manner, thus making it easily accessible to students. The last volume in the set contains primary source documents on the war. Suggested for both teachers and students.

McPherson, James M. *Battle Cry of Freedom*. New York: Oxford University Press, 1988.

> This is an excellent single-volume history of the Civil War. Written in a straightforward narrative style, the work nevertheless presents a comprehensive overview of the war and all its aspects. The Pulitizer-Prize winning book contains maps, photographs, and a bibliographical essay, as well as fully-documented footnotes. Because of its length, it is suggested for teachers and advanced students.

_____. *Ordeal By Fire*. New York: Alfred A. Knopf, 1982.

> Published as both a single volume and divided into three chronological volumes, this work provides a broad overview of the sectional crisis of the 19th century, the Civil War itself, and the era of Reconstruction. Suggested for both students and teachers.

Oates, Stephen B. *With Malice Toward None: A Life of Abraham Lincoln.* New York: Harper & Row, 1977.

> An excellent and well-written biography, this work looks at both Lincoln's private and public life to present a vital portrait of the man himself. Oates' book is well-researched and includes four dozen photographs of Lincoln, his family, friends, and colleagues. Recommended for teachers and advanced students.

Sandburg, Carl. *Storm Over the Land.* New York: Harcourt, Brace & Company, Inc., 1942.

> This is a one-volume abridgement of Mr. Sandburg's *Abraham Lincoln, The War Years.* Sandburg said of writing on the Civil War that one must "write till you are ashamed of yourself, and then cut it down next to nothing so the reader may hope beforehand he is not wasting his time." Though quite cut down, this is an effective one-volume treatment of the war. Some parts may seem dated to realists of the post-Vietnam era. Suggested for students and teachers.

Myers, Robert Manson, ed. *The Children of Pride.* New Haven: Yale University Press, 1972.

> This volume is a collection of letters giving the story of a family in the deep South in the 14 years bracketing the Civil War (1854-68). With the sense of immediacy and authenticity inherent in personal letters, this book documents Southern attitudes, social order, and reaction to events in this tumultuous era. Suggested for teachers as background reading and for upper-level students.

Young, Agatha. *Women and the Crisis.* New York: Ivan Obolensky, Inc., 1959.

> Young's book discusses the activities of Northern women during the war. As a result of the necessities imposed by the war, women gained a new sense of independence that was realized in the women's rights movements that followed. Suggested for students and teachers.

Camp Life

Gardner, Alexander. *Photographic Sketch Book of the Civil War.* Mineola, NY: Dover Publications, Inc., 1959.

> This collection, originally published in 1866, contains some of the finest work of the man many consider, in terms of technique, the finest photographer of the war period. The photographs range from relaxed portraits of groups of soldiers to ghastly battlefield shots. Accompanying text is very much in the rhetorical mode of the mid-19th century. Suggested for teachers and students.

Linderman, Gerald F. *Embattled Courage: The Experience of Combat in the American Civil War.* New York: Free Press, 1987.

> By taking a hard look at the life of ordinary soldiers in the Civil War, this work explores not only the experiences of the troops but attempts to explain why men fight when confronted with the horrors of warfare. Linderman looks at both soldiers' wartime experiences and their recollections of those experiences to reach his conclusions. He employs dozens of first-person narrative accounts in this book. Recommended for teachers and upper-level students.

Wiley, Bell Irwin. *Life of Johnny Reb.* Baton Rouge: Louisiana State University Press, 1978.

> An entertaining and enlighting portrayal of the everyday life of Confederate soldiers. In his preface, Wiley states his aim was to "present soldier life as it really was, and not as a thing of tradition...." This has been splendidly accomplished in this readable account. Recommended for high school students.

_____. *Life of Billy Yank.* Garden City, NY: Doubleday, 1971.

> This is the companion volume to Mr. Wiley's Johnny Reb, published 8 years earlier. This book is equally readable. The Union soldier is portrayed with all his strengths and frailties, as are his myriad motives for going to war and the wide range of experiences that followed his enlistment. Suggested for high school students.

Laborers, Contrabands, and Soldiers

Cornish, Dudley Taylor. *The Sable Arm*. Lawrence, KS: University Press of Kansas, 1987.

> On September 22, 1862, Abraham Lincoln issued the preliminary draft of the Emancipation Proclamation. As part of this proclamation, he authorized the enlistment of black troops. In retrospect, it seems he could hardly have done one without the other. For, as Cornish points out, it was the appearance of blacks in uniform that gave weight to the proclamation, that admitted blacks' ability to perform as soldiers, that "In short, (recognized) the Negro's manhood." Cornish documents the effects of enlistment of blacks on the North and South and on blacks and whites. Suggested for students and teachers.

Gerteis, Louis S. *From Contraband to Freedman*. Westport, CT: Greenwood Press, 1973.

> Gerteis' book traces the changes in federal policy towards blacks in the Civil War era. It is accepted by many that federal policy was dictated by altruism. Gerteis states here that necessities of war and a desire to gain black participation in the Northern war effort were more important factors than have previously been supposed. Suggested for teachers as background reading.

Litwack, Leon. *Been in the Storm So Long: The Aftermath of Slavery*. New York: Vintage Books, 1980.

> This volume focuses on the various experiences of blacks during and after the Civil War. It includes excerpts from diaries, slave interviews, and other primary sources. The first three chapters emphasize black experiences during the Civil War. Recommended as reference for students and teachers.

McPherson, James M. *The Negro's Civil War*. New York: Ballantine Books, 1991.

> In a biography of Gen. Ulysses S. Grant, Mr. W. E. Woodward stated "the American Negroes are the only people in the history of the world. . . that ever became free without any effort of their own...." McPherson's book effectively disputes this statement by documenting the large and varied role of blacks in the Northern war effort. Drawing heavily from speeches, letters, and diaries of prominent and unknown blacks of the period, McPherson tells of the black experience in the words of participants. Suggested for students and teachers.

War and Technology

Adams, George W. *Doctors in Blue*. Baton Rouge, La.: Louisiana State University Press, 1996.

> An account of the Northern response to the sickness and wounds generated by the Civil War, the book is a clear appraisal of medical and surgical techniques of the times and how successfully they were applied by Union doctors. It gives readers a clear understanding that the largest horrors of the Civil War may have been behind or beyond the battlefields, in sickbeds and makeshift hospitals. Suggested for teachers and students.

Bruce, Robert V. *Lincoln and the Tools of War*. Urbana, IL: University of Illinois Press, 1989.

> It is a piece of historical trivia that Abraham Lincoln was an amateur inventor before his presidency. Bruce explores this aspect of Lincoln's personality and how it manifested itself during the war. Here we see Lincoln as a major backer of some of the important innovations in weaponry of the period. Almost incidentally the book chronicles the effects of new ordnance on the Northern war effort. Suggested reading for students pursuing long-term projects on this topic.

Cunningham, H. H. *Doctors in Gray*. Baton Rouge, LA: Louisiana State University Press, 1993.

> This story of the Confederate medical service during the Civil War is also the story of a fledgling, would-be nation suffering from critical shortages of vital wartime necessities. The courageous and sometimes ingenious ways in which Southern medical officers responded to the conditions imposed upon them makes interesting reading. The shortcomings of Confederate surgeons and of the medical technology of the times are also examined. Suggested for teachers and upper-level high school students.

Davis, William C. *Duel Between the First Ironclads*. Mechanicsburg, PA: Stackpole Books, 1994.

> On March 9, 1862, two unique, iron-plated vessels met in the waters of Hampton Roads, VA. Both from a contemporary military standpoint and a larger technological perspective, it was to be an important day in naval history. Davis reports the exciting and improbable events leading up to this confrontation. He then traces the paths of the two iron warships in the battle's aftermath. Suggested for high school students.

Griffith, Paddy. *Battle Tactics of the Civil War*. New Haven: Yale University Press, 1987.

> Although many historians consider the Civil War as the first modern war, Griffith argues that it was actually the last to follow the pattern of warfare established by the Napoleonic Wars of the early 19th century. This book presents a detailed analysis of tactics and weaponry. Suggested for teachers only.

Grimsley, Mark. *The Hard Hand of War: Union Military Policy toward Southern Civilians, 1861-1865*. New York: Cambridge University Press, 1995.

> A detailed look at the Union Army's treatment of Southern civilians during the Civil War, Grimsley's book strips away the myths regarding Northern atrocities perpetuated against Southerners. Likewise, it also redefines the place of the Civil War in the larger academic discussion regarding "total war" and its evolution. With footnotes and an extensive bibliography, the work is well documented but very complicated. Recommended for teachers only.

Hagerman, Edward. *The American Civil War and the Origins of Modern Warfare: Ideas, Organization, and Field Command*. Bloomington: Indiana University Press, 1988.

> Hagerman's work argues that the Civil War was the first modern war, heralding such conflicts of the 20th century as World War I. He focuses specifically on how armies were organized and officered, as well as the early development of trench warfare and the advantage of holding the defensive position rather than the offensive. Recommended for teachers only.

Haydon, Frederick Stansbury. *Aeronautics in the Union and Confederate Armies*. Baltimore: Johns Hopkins University Press, 2000.

> This is an extensive and exhaustive study of the pioneer days of aerial warfare. The volume includes excellent illustrations, portraits of early innovators, and photographs and drawings of some of the first combat aircraft. Recommended to students pursuing long-term projects as suggested in this section.

Ball's Bluff

Blair, Harry C., and Tarshis, Rebecca. *The Life of Colonel Edward D. Baker*. Portland: Oregon Historical Society, 1960.

> This account deals with the colorful and far-ranging career of one of Abraham Lincoln's closest friends. From his emigration from England through life in frontier Illinois, election to the U.S. Senate from Oregon, to his controversial death in battle during the Civil War, Edward Baker's career loosely paralleled that of his adopted nation. Suggested as background reading for teachers and for students pursuing long-term projects.

Catton, Bruce. *Mr. Lincoln's Army*. New York: Anchor Books, 1990.

> This is the first book in Catton's trilogy on the Union Army of the Potomac. In chapter 2, part 2, he discusses the events surrounding the Battle of Ball's Bluff and the larger implications of that battle. Recommended for high school readers.

Johnson, R. U., et al., eds. *Battles and Leaders of the Civil War Vol II*. New York: The Century Co., 1887.

> This four-volume set contains reports, mostly by participating officers or eyewitnesses, of major military and diplomatic activities during the war. In Vol. II, Richard B. Irwin, who was an assistant adjutant general during the war, gives an intricate account of the Battle of Ball's Bluff and the subsequent arrest of Gen. Charles P. Stone. Suggested to teachers as background reading.

Sandburg, Carl. *Abraham Lincoln: The War Years*. New York: Harcourt, Brace & Company, Inc., 1939.

> In chapter 11 of volume 1 of this 4-volume set, Sandburg deals with the effects of Ball's Bluff on President Lincoln and the nation in general. Here, Sandburg discusses the special relationship between Lincoln and Edward Baker, "political" general killed at the battle, and the air of deep gloom that settled over the North in the battle's aftermath. Suggested for teachers and students.

Civilians and Government

Gray, Wood. *Hidden Civil War*. New York, The Viking Press, 1942.

> This is a story of the Copperheads, Northerners who were either opposed to the war from the outset or sickened by it as casualty rolls mounted and who sought to end it short of a Union victory. This book is useful in understanding the political currents at work in the 1860's. Suggested for teacher and upper-level students.

Smith, Edward Conrad. *The Borderland In the Civil War*. New York, AMS Press, 1970.

> In 1860 a broad strip of land, running from western Virginia roughly along the Ohio River to eastern Missouri and including parts of Ohio, Indiana and Illinois, separated the "true" North from the "true" South. Smith calls this belt "the Borderland." Citizens of these areas generally backed and fought for the Union, but for markedly different reasons than those in the industrial North. This book examines their social, economic, and political motives. Suggested for teachers and upper-level students.

Thomas, Emory M. *The Confederate Nation: 1861-1865*. New York: Harper & Row, 1979.

> An in-depth examination of the workings of the Confederate government over the course of the war, this book includes maps, photographs, and detailed footnotes. Emory discusses the contradictory forces working within the national government, between the national government and the military, and between the national and state governments to show how the Confederate war effort gradually disintegrated over the course of the war. Suggested for teachers.

Woodword, C. Vann, ed. *Mary Chesnut's Civil War*. New Haven: Yale University Press, 1981.

> This Pulitzer Prize-winning volume contains the wartime diary of Mary Chesnut, the wife of a prominent South Carolinian politician. Skillfully edited, Woodward allows Chesnut's poignant insights and lively wit to shine through while also providing readers with a moving description of life in the Confederacy from a woman's perspective over the course of the war. Since the book is long, it is suggested for teachers, who may want to present excerpts of the work to their students.

The Civil War: Soldiers and Civilians
Archival Citations of Documents

1. Letter from Hugh Garden to General E. A. Carman, regarding the battle of Sharpsburg (Antietam), May 1, 1896; Letters and Reports Concerning the Battle of Antietam, 1895-1900; "Antietam Studies"; Records of the Adjutant General's Office, 1780's-1917, Record Group 94; National Archives Building, Washington, DC.

2. Photograph No. NWDNS-111-B-3647 (Mathew Brady); "The inside of an officer's quarters during the Civil War," ca. 1860; Records of the Office of the Chief Signal Officer, Record Group 111; National Archives at College Park, College Park, MD.

3. Photograph No. NWDNS-111-B-0145 (Mathew Brady); "The camp of the 44th New York Volunteer Infantry near Alexandria, Virginia," ca. 1860; Records of the Office of the Chief Signal Officer, Record Group 111; National Archives at College Park, College Park, MD.

4. Photograph No. NWDNS-111-B-0359 (Mathew Brady); "Camp scene, Army of the Potomac," ca. 1860; Records of the Office of the Chief Signal Officer, Record Group 111; National Archives at College Park, College Park, MD.

5. Photograph No. NWDNS-111-B-5068 (Mathew Brady); "A group of the 22nd New York State Militia in full dress uniforms, encamped near Harper's Ferry, Virginia, 1862"; Records of the Office of the Chief Signal Officer, Record Group 111; National Archives at College Park, College Park, MD.

6. Photograph No. NWDNS-111-B-0289 (Mathew Brady); "A company of the 44th Indiana Volunteer Infantry taken in camp," ca. 1860; Records of the Office of the Chief Signal Officer, Record Group 111; National Archives at College Park, College Park, MD.

7. Photograph No. NWDNS-111-B-0216 (Mathew Brady); "Sutler store and soldier customers," ca. 1860; Records of the Office of the Chief Signal Officer, Record Group 111; National Archives at College Park, College Park, MD.

8. Price list for sutler's goods, February 7, 1863; Records of the Adjutant General's Office, 1780's-1917, Record Group 94; National Archives Building, Washington, DC.

9. Poster No. 45-x-9 (4x5 black & white negative); "The Conscript Bill! How To Avoid It!!," Navy recruiting poster, 1863; Records of the Department of Navy, Record Group 45; National Archives at College Park, College Park, MD.

10. Photograph No. NWDNS-111-B-2011 (Mathew Brady); "Crew portrait of the gunboat USS *Hunchback* at anchor in the James River, 1864"; Records of the Office of the Chief Signal Officer, Record Group 111; National Archives at College Park, College Park, MD.

11. Petition of Ned Baxter, Samuel Owens, and 43 others to Maj. Gen. Benjamin Butler, September 1864; Part I, series 5076; Department of Virginia and North Carolina, Army of the James; Records of U.S. Army Continental Commands, Record Group 393; National Archives Building, Washington, DC.

12. Photograph No. NWDNS-111-B-0400 (Mathew Brady); "Negro laborers at the Alexandria coal wharf," ca. 1860-1865; Records of the Office of the Chief Signal Officer, Record Group 111; National Archives at College Park, College Park, MD.

13. Petition from the colored citizens of Beaufort, NC, to Maj. Gen. Benjamin Butler, November 20, 1863; Part I, series 5076; Department of Virginia and North Carolina, Army of the James; Records of U.S. Army Continental Commands, 1821-1920, Record Group 393; National Archives Building, Washington, DC.

14. Protection of Colored Troops circular, 1863; File D-135; Enclosed in M.R. Delant to Secretary of War, December 15; Entry 360, Letters Received, Colored Troops Division; Records of the Adjutant General's Office, 1780's-1917, Record Group 94; National Archives Building, Washington, DC.

15. Petition from the officers commanding colored troops at Helena, AR, to the House and Senate requesting equal pay for their men, March 1864; Covering letter of S. Ex Doc 35, Letter of Agriculture Commission; Petition from 1st Iowa; 38th Congress, 2nd Session; Records of the U.S. Senate, Record Group 46; National Archives Building, Washington, DC.

16. Letter from Brig. Gen. Edwin Hinks to Maj. Gen. Benjamin Butler requesting the arming of his colored troops with the Spencer repeating rifle in place of their current unreliable weapons, April 29, 1864; Part II, no. 73, in Vol. 33/66 1/2 25AC, pp. 8-9; Entry 1659, Letters Sent, Department of Virginia and North Carolina; Records of U.S. Army Continental Commands, 1821-1920, Record Group 393; National Archives Building, Washington, DC.

17. Letter from Brig. Gen. Edwin Hinks to Maj. Gen. Benjamin Butler requesting investigation of the possible execution of captured colored soldiers under his command and retaliation against captured Confederate soldiers, May 28, 1864; Part I, LR H-192 (1864); Entry 5063, Department of Virginia and North Carolina; Records of U.S. Army Continental Commands, 1821-1920; Record Group 393; National Archives Building, Washington, DC.

18. Letter from Col. Hallowell, commanding the 54th Massachusetts Volunteer Infantry to John Andrews, governor of Massachusetts, explaining that his men will not accept any pay until their pay equals that of any other United States volunteer, November 23, 1863; Regimental Books and Papers, Letter Book (National Archives Microfilm Publication M1659, roll 1); 54th Massachusetts Volunteer Infantry (Colored Troops); Records of the Adjutant General's Office, 1780's-1917, Record Group 94; National Archives Building, Washington, DC.

19. Letter from John Bernabe and the free colored men of New Orleans to Maj. Gen. Nathanial Banks requesting permission to recruit and form the 5th Regiment, Louisiana Native Guards, March 11, 1863; Part I, Letter B-136 (1863); Entry 1920, Department of the Gulf; Records of U.S. Army Continental Commands, 1821-1920, Record Group 393; National Archives Building, Washington, DC.

20. Letter from Peter Cook of Baltimore, MD, to Army Adjutant General Brig. Gen. Lowell Thomas concerning the status of his three sons in the 30th Regiment of U. S. Colored Troops, November 7, 1864; 1863 A-Z, 1864 A-D, C-82; Colored Troops Division, Letters Relating to Recruiting, 1863-1868; Records of the Adjutant General's Office, 1780's-1917, Record Group 94; National Archives Building, Washington, DC.

21. Letter from Sarah Brown to Secretary of War Edwin Stanton requesting information about her husband, Samuel Brown, then serving in the 25th Regiment of U. S. Colored Troops, February 8, 1865; B-67; Colored Troops Division, Recruiting, 1864-1865; Records of the Adjutant General's Office, 1780's-1917, Record Group 94; National Archives Building, Washington, DC.

22. Letter from Mrs. Stevens to President Abraham Lincoln requesting discharge of her husband, Joseph Stevens, from his regiment of the U. S. Colored Troops, June 11, 1865; S-494; S-449-600, Colored Troops Division, 1865; Records of the Adjutant General's Office, 1780's-1917, Record Group 94; National Archives Building, Washington, DC.

23. Letter from Peter Peterson to Secretary of War Edwin Stanton requesting the back pay of his invalid brother, Samuel Peterson, to help pay the medical bills due after treating Samuel upon his return from Andersonville Prison, May 24, 1865; P-252; Entry 360, (1865); Records of the Adjutant General's Office, 1780's-1917, Record Group 94; National Archives Building, Washington, DC.

24. "Ball's Bluff...October 21, 1861," map showing positions of Union and Confederate Troops, by J. Wells; WDMC198-Virginia; Other records relating to civil functions; Records of the Office of the Chief of Engineers, Record Group 77; National Archives at College Park, College Park, MD.

25. Letter of transmittal from Maj. Gen. George McClellan to Secretary of War Simon Cameron reporting the engagement at Ball's Bluff, November 1, 1861; Unfolded and Flattened, Published in Official Records Volume 5; "Union Battle Reports" 1861-1865; Civil War Records Retained by the War Records Office, 1861-1865; Records of the Adjutant General's Office, 1780's-1917, Record Group 94; National Archives Building, Washington, DC.

26. Interim narration of the engagement at Ball's Bluff given by Brig. Gen. Charles Stone to his aide-de-camp , Col. Hardie, from his encampment at Poolesville, MD, December 2, 1861; Unfolded and Flattened, Published in Official Records Volume 5; "Union Battle Reports" 1861-1865; Civil War Records Retained by the War Records Office, 1861-1865; Records of the Adjutant General's Office, 1780's-1917; Record Group 94; National Archives Building, Washington, DC.

27. Narration of events of the engagement at Ball's Bluff written by Capt. Francis Young, of Col. Baker's staff, to Col. E. D. Townsend, October 28, 1861; Unfolded and Flattened, Published in Official Records Volume 5; "Union Battle Reports" 1861-1865; Civil War Records Retained by the War Records Office, 1861-1865; Records of the Adjutant General's Office, 1780's-1917, Record Group 94; National Archives Building, Washington, DC.

28. Report of the engagement at Ball's Bluff written by Brig. Gen. Nathan Evans, commanding the Confederate 7th Brigade, October 31, 1861; Vol. 4, pp. 348-353; Entry 4, Series 1, Official Records; War Department Collection of Confederate Records, Record Group 109; National Archives Building, Washington, DC.

29. Report of the engagement at Ball's Bluff written by Col. Edward Hinks, commanding the 19th Massachusetts Volunteer Infantry, to Brig. Gen. Lauder, October 23, 1861; Unfolded and Flattened, Published in Official Records Volume 5; "Union Battle Reports" 1861-1865; Civil War Records Retained by the War Records Office, 1861-1865; Records of the Adjutant General's Office, 1780's-1917, Record Group 94; National Archives Building, Washington, DC.

30. Drawing of Dr. Richard Gatling's "Revolving Battery Gun," patented November 4, 1862; Patent #36836; Utility Patent Drawings; Records of the Patent and Trademark Office, Record Group 241; National Archives at College Park, College Park, MD.

31. Drawing of "Ganster's Percussion Hand Grenade," October 24, 1864; July 1863-July 1869, Vol. 7, p. 62; Correspondence Regarding the Examination of Inventions, 1851-1880; Records of the Bureau of Ordnance, Record Group 74; National Archives Building, Washington, DC.

32. Letter from Ordnance Inspector William Jeffers to Com. H. G. Wise, Chief of the Bureau of Ordnance concerning testing of the Ganster Percussion Hand Grenade, October 24, 1864; July 1863-July 1869, Vol. 7, p. 61; Correspondence Regarding the Examination of Inventions, 1851-1880; Records of the Bureau of Ordnance, Record Group 74; National Archives Building, Washington, DC.

33. Letter from Lt. Com. William Mitchell to Capt. John Adolphus Dahlgren, Chief of the Bureau of Ordnance concerning the testing of Hyde's War Rockets in the presence of President Abraham Lincoln and other distinguished visitors, November 18, 1862.; February 1861-July 1863, Vol. 4, p. 215; Correspondence Regarding the Examination of Inventions, 1851-1880; Records of the Bureau of Ordnance, Record Group 74; National Archives Building, Washington, DC.

34. Page 19 of *General Index of Patents*, 1790-1873; Subject Matter of Patents for Inventions issued by the United States Patent Office, 1790-1873 (Compiled by M.D. Leggett); Volume 1, p. 19; Records of the Patent and Trademark Office, Record Group 241; National Archives at College Park, College Park, MD.

35. Page 22 of *General Index of Patents*, 1790-1873; Subject Matter of Patents for Inventions by the United States Patent Office, 1790-1873 (Compiled by M.D. Leggett); Volume 1, p. 22; Records of the Patent and Trademark Office, Record Group 241; National Archives at College Park, College Park, MD.

36. Excerpt from *Introduction to the Medical and Surgical History of the War of the Rebellion* concerning the effect the war had on advancing medical knowledge of treating wounds and injuries; *Introduction to the Medical and Surgical History of the War of the Rebellion*, pp. XXVIII and XXVIX, Washington, D. C., Government Printing Office, 1870; Records of the Adjunct General's Office, 1780's-1917, Record Group 94; National Archives Building, Washington, DC.

37. Letter from Assistant Surgeon J. Theodore Calhoun concerning the treatment of a gunshot wound in the forearm during the Battle of Chancellorsville, August 26, 1863; Entries 623-631; Records of the Adjutant General's Office, 1780's-1917, Record Group 94; National Archives Building, Washington, DC.

38. Case history of 1st Sgt. George W. Clark, 30th New York, wounded by two gunshot wounds in the right leg at the Battle of Second Bull Run, August 30, 1862; Entries 623-631; Records of the Adjutant General's Office, 1780's-1917, Record Group 94; National Archives Building, Washington, DC.

39. Letter from Lt. Col. John Billings to Mr. L. Casella inquiring about the purchase of clinical thermometers for distribution to medical officers in the U. S. Army, May 1864; Entries 623-631; Records of the Adjutant General's Office, 1780's-1917, Record Group 94; National Archives Building, Washington, DC.

40. Case history of Pvt. Philip Fitzsimmons, 2nd U. S. Cavalry from his wounding at the Battle of Brandy Station on August 1, 1863, until his death by tetanus on August 14, 1863, including all treatments written by Assistant Surgeon W. Thomson; Entries 623-631; Records of the Adjutant General's Office, 1780's-1917, Record Group 94; National Archives Building, Washington, DC.

41. Drawing of Patent 44643, "E. R. McKean's Improved Ambulance," October 11, 1864; Patent #44643; Utility Patent Drawings; Records of the Patent and Trademark Office, Record Group 241; National Archives at College Park, College Park, MD.

42. Drawing of Patent 37667, Thomas Shaw's Improvement in Aerostation, patented February 10, 1863; Patent #37667; Utility Patent Drawings; Records of the Patent and Trademark Office, Record Group 241; National Archives at College Park, College Park, MD.

43. Letter from Col. E. W. Marsh to Col. J. O. Broadhead concerning the arrest of editor H. Lick of "The Rolla Express," October 15, 1863; (National Archives Microfilm Publication M345, Lick, H.); War Department Collection of Confederate Records, Record Group 109; National Archives Building, Washington, DC.

44. Letter from Col. Martin Bush to Brig. Gen. Boyle seeking compensation for losses on his farm due to a visit from Col. John Morgan's unit, June 31, 1863; (National Archives Microfilm Publication M345, Bush, M.M.); War Department Collection of Confederate Records, Record Group 109; National Archives Building, Washington, DC.

45. Order 883, ordering the transfer of one Henry Buster from the Chief of City Police in St. Louis, MO, to the military prison, June 21, 1862. He is charged with "hurrahing for Jeff Davis"; (National Archives Microfilm Publication M345, Buster, Henry); War Department Collection of Confederate Records, Record Group 109; National Archives Building, Washington, DC.

46. Excerpt from the October 10, 1863, edition of "The Rolla Express"; (National Archives Microfilm Publication M345, Lick, H.); War Department Collection of Confederate Records, Record Group 109; National Archives Building, Washington, DC.

47. Presidential Proclamation No. 94, suspending the writ of habeas corpus, September 24, 1862; (National Archives Microfilm Publication M345); War Department Collection of Confederate Records, Record Group 109; National Archives Building, Washington, DC.

48. Journal entry of the Special Commission convened in St. Louis, MO, December 11, 1863, concerning the improper arrest of John Bush; (National Archives Microfilm Publication M345, Bush, John); War Department Collection of Confederate Records, Record Group 109; National Archives Building, Washington, DC.

49. Statement of W. D. Richardson concerning the anti-Union guerilla activities of Joseph and John Hedge[s], given on November 16, 1864; (National Archives Microfilm Publication M345, Hedge, Joseph); War Department Collection of Confederate Records, Record Group 109; National Archives Building, Washington, DC.

50. Letter from Fannie Dent to Capt. Charles Fletcher, 1st U. S. Infantry, seeking the release of her brother, Joseph Hedges, December 1864; (National Archives Microfilm Publication M345, Hedge, Joseph); War Department Collection of Confederate Records, Record Group 109; National Archives Building, Washington, DC.

51. Letter from Livania Hedges to Col. Maxwell seeking the release of her husband, November 28, 1864; (National Archives Microfilm Publication M345, Hedge, Joseph); War Department Collection of Confederate Records, Record Group 109; National Archives Building, Washington, DC.

52. Oath of allegiance to the Union signed by J. P. Bush of Monroe County, MO, March 3, 1862; (National Archives Microfilm Publication M345, Bush, J.P.); War Department Collection of Confederate Records, Record Group 109; National Archives Building, Washington, DC.

53. Letter from C. Brown concerning the loyalty of Mrs. Ann Bush, October 12, 1861; (National Archives Microfilm Publication M345); War Department Collection of Confederate Records, Record Group 109; National Archives Building, Washington, DC.

54. Excerpt of the charges and specifications lodged against H. Lick, editor of "The Rolla Express," October 10, 1863; (National Archives Microfilm Publication M345, Lick, H.); War Department Collection of Confederate Records, Record Group 109; National Archives Building, Washington, DC.

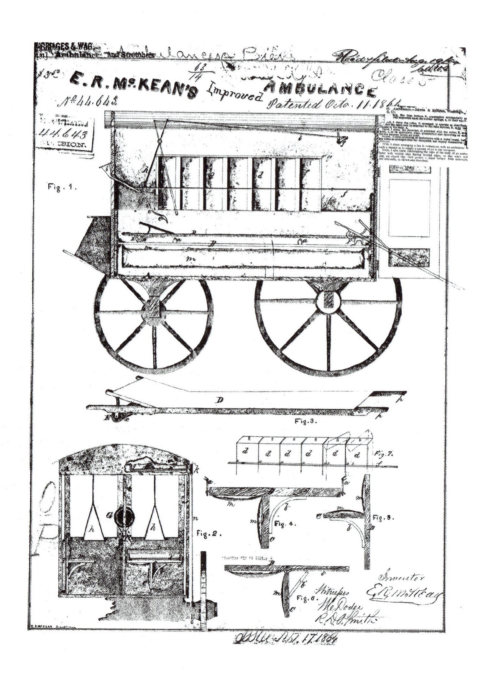

About the National Archives:
A Word to Educators

The National Archives and Records Administration (NARA) is responsible for the preservation and use of the permanently valuable records of the federal government. These materials provide evidence of the activities of the government from 1774 to the present in the form of written and printed documents, maps and posters, sound recordings, photographs, films, computer tapes, and other media. These rich archival sources are useful to everyone: federal officials seeking information on past government activities, citizens needing data for use in legal matters, historians, social scientists and public policy planners, environmentalists, historic preservationists, medical researchers, architects and engineers, novelists and playwrights, journalists researching stories, students preparing papers, and persons tracing their ancestry or satisfying their curiosity about particular historical events. These records are useful to you as educators either in preparing your own instructional materials or pursuing your own research.

The National Archives records are organized by the governmental body that created them rather than under a library's subject/author/title categories. There is no Dewey decimal or Library of Congress designation; each departmental bureau or collection of agency's records is assigned a record group number. In lieu of a card catalog, inventories and other finding aids assist the researcher in locating material in records not originally created for research purposes, often consisting of thousands of cubic feet of documentation.

The National Archives is a public institution whose records and research facilities nationwide are open to anyone 14 years of age and over. These facilities are found in the Washington, DC, metropolitan area, in the 11 Presidential libraries, the Nixon Presidential Materials Project, and in 16 regional archives across the nation. Whether you are pursuing broad historical questions or are interested in the history of your family, admittance to the research room at each location requires only that you fill out a simple form stating your name, address, and research interest. A staff member then issues an identification card, which is good for two years.

If you come to do research, you will be offered an initial interview with a reference archivist. You will also be able to talk with archivists who have custody of the records. If you have a clear definition of your questions and have prepared in advance by reading as many of the secondary sources as possible, you will find that these interviews can be very helpful in guiding you to the research material you need.

The best printed source of information about the overall holdings of the National Archives is the *Guide to the National Archives of the United States* (issued in 1974, reprinted in 1988), which is available in university libraries and many public libraries and online at **www.nara.gov**. The *Guide* describes in very general terms the records in the National Archives, gives the background and history of each agency represented by those records, and provides useful information about access to the records. To accommodate users outside of Washington, DC, the regional archives hold microfilm copies of much that is found in Washington. In addition, the regional archives contain records created by field offices of the federal government, including district and federal appellate court records, records of the Bureau of Indian Affairs, National Park Service, Bureau of Land Management, Forest Service, Bureau of the Census, and others. These records are particularly useful for local and regional history studies and in linking local with national historical events.

For more information about the National Archives and its educational and cultural programs, visit NARA's Web site at **www.nara.gov**.

Presidential Libraries

Herbert Hoover Library
210 Parkside Drive
West Branch, IA 52358-0488
319-643-5301

Franklin D. Roosevelt Library
511 Albany Post Road
Hyde Park, NY 12538-1999
914-229-8114

Harry S. Truman Library
500 West U.S. Highway 24
Independence, MO 64050-1798
816-833-1400

Dwight D. Eisenhower Library
200 Southeast Fourth Street
Abilene, KS 67410-2900
785-263-4751

John Fitzgerald Kennedy Library
Columbia Point
Boston, MA 02125-3398
617-929-4500

Lyndon Baines Johnson Library
2313 Red River Street
Austin, TX 78705-5702
512-916-5137

Gerald R. Ford Library
1000 Beal Avenue
Ann Arbor, MI 48109-2114
734-741-2218

Jimmy Carter Library
441 Freedom Parkway
Atlanta, GA 30307-1498
404-331-3942

Ronald Reagan Library
40 Presidential Drive
Simi Valley, CA 93065-0600
805-522-8444/800-410-8354

George Bush Library
1000 George Bush Drive
P.O. Box 10410
College Station, TX 77842-0410
409-260-9552

Clinton Presidential Materials Project
1000 LaHarpe Boulevard
Little Rock, AR 72201
501-254-6866

National Archives Regional Archives

NARA-Northeast Region
380 Trapelo Road
Waltham, MA 02452-6399
781-647-8104

NARA-Northeast Region
10 Conte Drive
Pittsfield, MA 01201-8230
413-445-6885

NARA-Northeast Region
201 Varick Street, 12th Floor
New York, NY 10014-4811
212-337-1300

NARA-Mid Atlantic Region
900 Market Street
Philadelphia, PA 19107-4292
215-597-3000

NARA-Mid Atlantic Region
14700 Townsend Road
Philadelphia, PA 19154-1096
215-671-9027

NARA-Southeast Region
1557 St. Joseph Avenue
East Point, GA 30344-2593
404-763-7474

NARA-Great Lakes Region
7358 South Pulaski Road
Chicago, IL 60629-5898
773-581-7816

NARA-Great Lakes Region
3150 Springboro Road
Dayton, OH 45439-1883
937-225-2852

NARA-Central Plains Region
2312 East Bannister Road
Kansas City, MO 64131-3011
816-926-6272

NARA-Central Plains Region
200 Space Center Drive
Lee's Summit, MO 64064-1182
816-478-7079

NARA-Southwest Region
501 West Felix Street
P.O. Box 6216
Fort Worth, TX 76115-0216
817-334-5525

NARA-Rocky Mountain Region
Denver Federal Center, Building 48
P.O. Box 25307
Denver, CO 80225-0307
303-236-0804

NARA-Pacific Region
24000 Avila Road
P.O. Box 6719
Laguna Niguel, CA 92607-6719
949-360-2641

NARA-Pacific Region
1000 Commodore Drive
San Bruno, CA 94066-2350
650-876-9009

NARA-Pacific Alaska Region
6125 Sand Point Way, NE
Seattle, WA 98115-7999
206-526-6507

NARA-Pacific Alaska Region
654 West Third Avenue
Anchorage, AK 99501-2145
907-271-2443

Reproductions of Documents

Reproductions of the oversized print documents included in these units are available in their original size by special order from Graphic Visions.

HUGH R. GARDEN,
Counsellor at Law,
Mutual Life Building,
NEW YORK.

New York M a y 1st 1896.

Gen. E. A. Carman,
    Sharpsburg, Maryland.
My dear Sir:-

Replying to your letter of April twenty-fourth, I hand you to be attached to the map, which you sent to me, such memoranda relating to the movements and services of my battery at Antietam, as my memory will afford after a lapse of thirty-three years.

The Palmetto Light Battery, six twelve lb. howitzers, Capt. Hugh R. Garden, familiarly known as Garden's Battery, moved with the rear guard of Gen. Lee's Army from Boonsboro Gap, Maryland to Sharpsburg on the night of the fifteenth of September 1862, and in the early morning of the sixteenth, Garden's Battery was ordered into position on the Heights, immediately in front of the Town of Sharpsburg between the Boonsboro Main Road, and the Country road running from Sharpsburg to and crossing Burnside's Bridge and supposed to command the Bridge.

The two heavy red marks on the map indicate the position taken by this Battery during that day.

Not a shot was fired on the sixteenth; and the night of the sixteenth was spent in the Valley in an apple orchard, as indicated by the heavy black mark on the map.

On the morning of the seventeenth position was again taken on the top of the Heights as indicated by the heavy red marks. The location being very conspicuous afforded a target for the artillery of long range on the opposite side of Antietam Creek, in full view but beyond the range of the guns of Garden's Battery.

While subjected to this artillery fire, one gun of Garden's Battery was dismounted by a shot striking an axle. Another gun was disabled by a shot in the mouth of the Cannon.

Lieutenant S. M. Pringle was mortally wounded. Sergeant James Henry Rice and several Privates were wounded and a number of horses killed. The fire of Garden's Battery was directed entirely against the massing of Burnside's Corps at the Bridge crossing, and while preparing for their subsequent advance on the South side of Antietam Creek, and also during their advance across the plateau after crossing the Creek, and while assending the range of hills on which this Battery was located.

The only Confederate Infantry in sight until late in the afternoon of the 17th was a regiment of South Carolians, I think commanded by Col. F. W. McMaster, which extended across the

Document 1a. Letter to Gen. E. A. Carman from Hugh Garden, May 1, 1896. [National Archives]

HUGH R. GARDEN,
Counsellor at Law,
Mutual Life Building,
NEW YORK.

New York _____ No. 2. E.A.C. 189

Valley in which the apple orchard was located; and which was, as I recollect, mainly deployed as sharpshooters in that Valley. I remember that Major E. B. Cantey of that regiment was wounded twice in the apple orchard.

The advance of Burnside's Corps was therefore practically unimpeded, except by the fire from these guns and a small body of skirmishers, and they were upon the slope of the eminence occupied by Garden's Battery, and had swept around his right and rear, when the opportune appearance of Stonewall Jackson's troops immediately on the right, across the little valley, and beyond the apple orchard. ~~These command swept over the hill.~~ checked Burnside's people, and enabled me as the day closed to withdraw all of my wounded and also the two disabled guns.

At the time that Jackson's troops advanced, the enemy were almost in the rear of the Battery on the right and in the apple orchard, and the Battery had actually begun its retreat with the danger of speedy capture in the Streets of the Town behind it.

Lieutenant Pringle, who had been taken into a house under the hill, immediately behind the Battery, was with his litter-bearers in the midst of a sharp Infantry fight as my Battery moved away.

If I had any means of refreshing my memory, I might give you some further information, but I suppose that the foregoing is sufficient for your purpose.

Very respectfully,

Hugh R Garden

Document 1b. Letter to Gen. E. A. Carman from Hugh Garden, May 1, 1896. [National Archives]

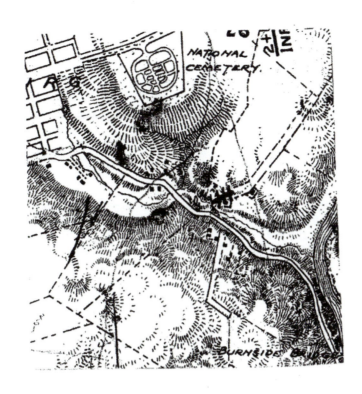

Lt J Harvey Wilson says Garden's Batty when it arrived on Sep 15 filed to the left on crest of hill. The first night and day parked in ravine and pear orchard about G. When time was formed was placed on top of hill fronting Burnside Bridge and action was with Burnside's advance (Red mark) A few yards to right say 30 was a precipitous bluff to the ravine in which we had been parked. A spring and spring house (Tennants) in this ravine, and the orchard was about 100 yards south of the spring house. No artillery on the right. Fought Burnside and Batty E 4th U.S. Arty. In the rear probably 40 yds was a somewhat precipitous, rocky elevation to a higher hill or a more elevated point of same hill.

Wilson lives at Maysville, S.C.

Document 1c. Letter to Gen. E. A. Carman from Hugh Garden, May 1, 1896. [National Archives]

Document 2. Photograph by Mathew Brady, "The inside of an officer's quarters during the Civil War," ca. 1860. [National Archives]

Document 3. Photograph by Mathew Brady, "The camp of the 44th New York Volunteer Infantry near Alexandria, Virginia," ca. 1860. [National Archives]

Document 4. Photograph by Mathew Brady, "Camp scene, Army of the Potomac," ca. 1860. [National Archives]

Document 5. Photograph by Mathew Brady, "A group of the 22nd New York State Militia in full dress uniforms, encamped near Harper's Ferry, Virginia," 1862. [National Archives]

Document 6. Photograph by Mathew Brady, "A company of the 44th Indiana Volunteer Infantry taken in camp," ca. 1860. [National Archives]

Document 7. Photograph by Mathew Brady, "Sutler store
and soldier customers," ca. 1860. [National Archives]

Saturday February 7ᵗʰ 1863

The Council met according to adjournment and proceeded to fix the following prices of Sutlers Goods, & others named in the above order. Present Capt J. T. Cotton & Capt A. W. Rollins.

Dry & Fancy Goods, Stationery &c.

Item			Price
Madder Handkerchief		Each	30
Gingham		"	25
Pongee	Cotton	"	38
Pongee	Silk		75
Fancy Hose	Mens	Per pair	20
Brown "	"	"	20
Cotton "	"	"	25
Suspenders		"	50
Fancy Mirrors			38 to 62
Buckskin Purses			50 to 75
Wallets			50 to 72
Port Monaies		Each	75
Hair Brushes		"	50
Tooth do		"	25
Dress Combs		"	25
Linen Cambric H'dkfs			57 to 62
Musquitoe Bars		"	2 00
White Cotton Gloves		Per pair	15
Spool Cotton		" Spool	10
Needles		" Paper	10
Mens Slippers		" pair	1 75
Balmorals		" " 2.50 to 5	00
Tumblers & Goblets		" Doz 1.50 to 2	50
Dining Plates		" " 1.50 to 2	00
Coffee Cups & Saucers		" Set	1 25
Tea " "		" "	62
Pitchers		Each	50 to 75
Bowls		"	12 to 15
Army Knives & Forks			1 50
Water pails		Each	40

Document 8a. Excerpt from price list of sutler's goods, February 7, 1863. [National Archives]

Razors		Each	75cts to	1 00
do Strops		"		25
Paper Collars		"		04
Letter Paper		Per Quire		20
" Commercial Note				20
Envelopes		Per Bunch		10 to 20
Ink		" bottle		18

Canned Articles

Mutton	Per Can	2 lbs			1 00
Lobster	"	"	1	"	38
"	"	"	2	"	75
Roast Beef		"	"		1 00
Green Peas			1	"	50
" Corn			2	"	88
Pine Apple			3	"	1 00
Strawberries		"	"		1 00
Raspberries			2	"	1 00
Jellies		Per cup			45
Preserves		" jar			50 to 75
Chow Chow		" bottle			62

Groceries, Provisions & Fruits

Butter	Per pound		40
Cheese	" "		20
Ham	" "		10
" Canvassed	" "		12
Mackerel	" Kit		1 50
Cod fish	" pound		10
Ground Coffee	" "		40
Candles, Adamantine	" "		40
Raisins	" "		30
Sugar	" "		20 to 25
Flour	" "		08
"	" barrel		15 00
Soap	" bar		25
" Castile	" pound		50

Document 8b. Excerpt from price list of sutler's goods, February 7, 1863. [National Archives]

THE CONSCRIPT BILL!

HOW TO AVOID IT!!

U. S. NAVY.

1,000 MEN WANTED, FOR 12 MONTHS!

Seamen's Pay,	$18.00	per month.
Ordinary Seamen's Pay,	14.00	" "
Landsmen's Pay,	12.00	" "

$1.50 extra per month to all, Grog Money.

$50,000,000 PRIZES!

Already captured, a large share of which is awarded to Ships Crews.   The laws for the distributing of Prize money carefully protects the rights of all the captors.

PETTY OFFICERS,—PROMOTION.—Seamen have a chance for promotion to the offices of Master at Arms, Boatswain's Mates, Quarter Gunners, Captain of Tops, Forecastle, Holds, After-Guard, &c.

Landsmen may be advanced to Armorers, Armorers' Mates, Carpenter's Mates, Sailmakers' Mates, Painters, Coopers, &c.

PAY OF PETTY OFFICERS,—From $20.00 to $45.00 per month.

CHANCES FOR WARRANTS, BOUNTIES AND MEDALS OF HONOR.—All those who distinguish themselves in battle or by extraordinary heroism, may be promoted to forward Warrant Officers or Acting Masters' Mates,—and upon their promotion receive a guaranty of $100, with a medal of honor from their country.

All who wish may leave HALF PAY with their families, to commence from date of enlistment.

Minors must have a written consent, sworn to before a Justice of the Peace.

For further information apply to U. S. NAVAL RENDEZVOUS,

E. Y. BUTLER, U. S. N. Recruiting Officer,

No. 14 FRONT STREET, SALEM, MASS.

FROM WRIGHT & POTTER'S BOSTON PRINTING ESTABLISHMENT, No. 4 SPRING LANE, CORNER OF DEVONSHIRE STREET.

Document 9. Poster, "The Conscript Bill! How To Avoid It!!," 1863. [National Archives]

Document 10. Photograph, scene on deck of gunboat Hunchback, 1864. [National Archives]

Bermuda Hundred's V.A. Septm 1864

To Major Genl. Butler

Sir, you will pardon us for troubling you with this report but knowing you to be a Gentleman of Justice and a friend to the Negro race in this Country, we take the liberty to send you the following facts.

Forty five of us Colored people, worked for four months throughing up breast work's at Roanoke Island. Augt 31st we were told to report at head quarters to be paid. we went according to orders, when we got there, a guard of soldiers was put over us, and we marched on board a steamer, at the point of the bayonet; we were told the pay master was on board the steamer, to pay us. then we was to go to Fortress Munroe. then told that we was going to Dutch Gap to be paid. true we was on the way to Dutch Gap to work on the canal.

guards were then sent over the Island to take up every man that could be found, indiscriminately young and old sick and well, the soldiers broke into the coulored people's house's taken sick men out of bed. men that had sick wives, and men

Document 11a. Petition of Ned Baxter, Samuel Owens, and 43 others to Maj. Gen. Benjamin Butler, September 1864. [National Archives]

that had large family's of children and no wife or person to cut wood for them or take care of them, were taken, and not asked one question or word about going, had we been asked to go to dutch gap a large number would have gone without causeing the suffering, that has been caused, we are willing to go where our labour is wanted and we are ready at any time to do all we can for the goverment at any place and feel it our duty, to help the goverment all we can, but goverment dont know the treatment we receive from Supts of Contrabands.

we have not been paid for our work don at Roanoke, consequently our wives and family's are there suffering for clothes, Captn James has paid us for only two months work this year, the months of Febuary and January, No one knows the injustice practiced on the negro's at Roanoke, our garden's are plundered by the white soldiers. what we raise to surport our selves with is stolen from us, and if we say any thing about it we are sent to the guard house, rations that the goverment allows the contrabands are sold to the white secech Citizen's, and got out the way at night, its no uncommon thing to see weman and children crying for something to eat, Old clothes sent to the Island from the North for contrabands are sold to the white secesh citizen's. by the asst. Superintendant Mr Sanderson.

Genl. these thing's are not gessed at but things that can be proved by those that saw them. and many more things that we can prove. Captn James. does not look after things. so Mr Sanderson has his own way he now talk's of sending two hundred weman from Roanoke. then our family's will be sent one way and we in another direction. most of the weman there are soldiers wives sent there by Genl. Wild for protection. must they be sent away when their husbands are in the army fighting. we humbley ask you to look into these things. and do some thing for the negro's at Roanoke Island

　　　　we remain your humble servants

Ned Baxter working for Captn Walbridge A. A. Q. M.
　　　　　　　Bermuda 100's
　　　　　1st Bry 3 Dev 18 A. Corps Wilsons landing
Saml Owen's working for Captn Bayley 37 U. S. Co Troops
And forty three other contrabands
from Roanoke Island N. C.

Document 12. Photograph by Mathew Brady, "Negro laborers
at Alexandria," ca.1860-1865. [National Archives]

To Maj Gen! B. F. Butler.
Commanding Department of Virginia
&c North Carolina.

the undersigned
Colored Citizens of the town of Beaufort in
behalf of the Colored population of this Community
in view of the manner in which their Brothers are
oppressed by the military authorities in this Vicinity
Respeckfuley pittision You are at the Head of this Military
Department for a redress of grievences

Your politiness desire to make known
to You that they and their brothern   to the
President of the United States are undiscriminatly
impressed by the authorities to labor upon the
Public woorks without Compensation that in
Consequence of this System of fource labor they
Have no means of paying Rents and otherwise
Providing for ther families

Your pittisioners desire further to Express
ther Entire Willingness to Contribute to the Cause of
the union in anyway Consistant with their Cause
as Freemen and the Rights of their families

Anything that can Be don By
You to relieve us from the Burden which wee are
Now Labooring will Be Highly Appreciated By
Your Petitiorns
Peter Henry And Your pititioners will Ever pray
Charles henry
Enock Miller   Beaufort N. Caroline
C. H. W. Henderson   Nov 20th 1863
Goson Gaskill
                       Yours Respeckfully & Soforth —

COLORED SOLDIERS!

EQUAL STATE RIGHTS!
AND MONTHLY PAY WITH WHITE MEN!!

On the 1st day of January, 1863, the President of the United States proclaimed

FREEDOM TO OVER

THREE MILLIONS OF SLAVES!

This decree is to be enforced by all the power of the Nation.   On the 21st of July last he issued the following order:—

PROTECTION OF COLORED TROOPS.

" WAR DEPARTMENT, ADJUTANT GENERAL'S OFFICE, }
WASHINGTON, July 21. }

" *General Order, No. 233.*

" The following order of the President is published for the information and government of all concerned :—

EXECUTIVE MANSION, WASHINGTON, July 30.

' " It is the duty of every Government to give protection to its citizens, of whatever class, color, or condition, and especially to those who are duly organized as soldiers in the public service.   The law of nations, and the usages and customs of war, as carried on by civilized powers, permit no distinction as to color in the treatment of prisoners of war as public enemies.   To sell or enslave any captured person on account of his color, is a relapse into barbarism, and a crime against the civilization of the age.

' " The Government of the United States will give the same protection to all its soldiers, and if the enemy shall sell or enslave any one because of his color, the offence shall be punished by retaliation upon the enemy's prisoners in our possession.   It is, therefore, ordered, for every soldier of the United States, killed in violation of the laws of war, a rebel soldier shall be executed; and for every one enslaved by the enemy, or sold into slavery, a rebel soldier shall be placed at hard labor on the public works, and continued at such labor until the other shall be released and receive the treatment due to prisoners of war.

' " ABRAHAM LINCOLN." '

' " By order of the Secretary of War.

' " E. D. TOWNSEND, Assistant Adjutant General." '

That the President is in earnest the rebels soon began to find out, as witness the following order from his Secretary of War :—

" WAR DEPARTMENT, WASHINGTON CITY, August 8, 1863.

" SIR :—Your letter of the 3d inst., calling the attention of this Department to the cases of Orin H. Brown, William H. Johnston, and Wm. Wilson, three colored men captured on the gunboat Isaac Smith, has received consideration.   This Department has directed that three rebel prisoners of South Carolina, if there be any such in our possession, and if not, three others, be confined in close custody and held as hostages for Brown, Johnston, and Wilson, and that the fact be communicated to the rebel authorities at Richmond.

" Very respectfully your obedient servant,

" EDWIN M. STANTON, Secretary of War.

" The Hon. GIDEON WELLES, Secretary of the Navy."

And retaliation will be our practice now—man for man—to the bitter end.

To the Honorable, the
Senate & House of Representatives
of the American Congress

Gentlemen.
The
Officers of the Negro Troops sta
tioned at the Post of Helena
Ark. would, most respectfully
draw your attention to a few
facts and considerations respecting
the enlisted men under our
Command.

In securing to many of
these men, personal freedom
the Government has at once
performed an act of justice,
and bestowed a great boon.

In organizing and arming
them, a timely and potent
instrumentality has been em
ployed for the punishment of
treason, and the re-establishment
and perpetuity of the wisest
and most beneficent government
ever bestowed upon man.

We regret, however, that

complete provision has not hitherto been made for the suitable compensation of these Patriot Citizen Soldiers of African Descent.

But we greatly rejoice to observe a manifest disposition on your part, as the Honorable Representatives of the Loyal People of the nation to supply this deficiency.

On behalf of the men whom we have the honor to command, their wives and children, we must earnestly petition your Honorable Body to enact a law securing to them, for their entire term of service, the same pay & emoluments as are now provided for United States Soldiers, not of African Descent.

This we deem,

1st. A Demand of Equity.

These men have voluntarily taken up arms, in a time of great public peril for the defense of the Government and the vindication of our common country's flag.

To do this many of them have abandoned home, and all of domestic happiness they possessed; made tedious marches through mud & Snow; lying in the woods for days, sometimes for weeks, in a half starving condition: hunted by the enemy, or the no less despicable slave driving pretenders to loyalty, with guns and hounds. In a partially starved & frozen condition, they have reached the places of rendezvous, and manfully entered upon the duty of Soldiers.

We know of no instance in which Negro Soldiers have disgraced themselves in action, In a number of instances their bravery & daring have challenged the admiration of the entire country; and extorted from their bitterest enemies, the concession that they possess pluck & capacity.

We believe the measure of drill and discipline attained by these troops. Equal to that of white troops in the same length of time; and it must be allowed without controversy that the amount of fatigue duty performed by them is far greater than that performed by the same number of the other class.

2d. What we ask is required by sound policy.

These men have reposed the utmost confidence in the integrity and liberality of the Government.

It is not well that this confidence be shaken or destroyed.

With the clearest insight into the relationship subsisting between and the obligations and duties of all the parties concerned, these men have, thus far, with rare exceptions, borne faithfully and cheerfully all the dis— abilities devolved upon them.

Now however, they feel that the time has fully come for their complete enfranchisement as American Soldiers.

Document 15d. Petition of officers of Negro troops stationed at Port Helena, AR, to the Senate and House of Representatives, March 1864. [National Archives]

This they ask and expect.

We, their officers ask and expect it for them.

Let us, we pray you, have an enactment by the present Congress, meeting these demands and thrilling the hearts of these patriots with renewed confidence and courage.

Such a provision by Congress would induce the speedy enlistment of all the Negroes within reach of our lines, and place in the hands of every officer bearing a Commission to command them, the means of bringing them, speedily, to the highest practicable standard of soldierly attainment and duty.

Names.

John G. Hudson, Col. Comdg 1st Regt Iowa Vols Infty A.D.

Milton H. Collins Lat. Col 1st Iowa Vols Infty A.D

John L. Murphy Maj 1st Iowa Vols Infty A.D.

Wm. McQueen Lt & R.Q.M 1st Iowa vols Inft A.D

William Knowles Surgn 1st Iowa Infantry A.D.

Andrew Patton asst Surg 1st Iowa Infantry A.D.

Head Quarters of Division
Camp Hamilton Va
April 29" 1864

Butler B. F.

14

Maj General B F Butler
Comdg Dept of Va & N.C.
                                    General,
                                            In view
of the approaching campaign, and more
especially on account of the recent inhuman-
ities of the enemy perpetrated upon troops
of like character to those of my command,
I deem it my duty to urge that these
troops shall be more efficiently armed, to
enable them to defend themselves and lessen
their liability to capture.

                        There certainly
out to be no objection to arming these troops
with as effective a weapon as any that are
placed in the hands of white Soldiers, who are
to go into battle with none of the peculiar
disadvantages to which my men will be subject

                        The present arms of several regiments
in the division are inferior, in kind and manufacture.

                        The Springfield Rifled musket of the
Bridesburg manufacture is an unreliable gun.
The contract Enfield Rifle is also unreliable;
and one Regt is armed with the Old Harpers
Ferry smoothbore.

Document 16a. Letter to Maj. Gen. Benjamin Butler from Edwin Hinks
on the subject of arms, April 29, 1864. [National Archives]

Now these arms will perhaps answer for troops who will be well cared for if they fall into his hands, But to troops who cannot afford to be beaten, and will not be taken, the best arm should be given that the country can afford.

The retaliation we should at present adopt is to arm our colored troops with Spencers Repeating Rifle, and I request that my Division or a part of them may be armed with a repeating or breech-loading fire arm

I am General:
Very Respectfully
Your Obt Servt

Brig Genl Comdg

Head Quarters Hink's Division
City Point Va May 28th 1864

Maj Genl B. F. Butler
   Comdg Dept Va and N.C.
     In the Field

        General—

It is reported that on Sunday the 22nd inst; two men of the 22nd U.S.C Infantry, who were captured by the enemy on the 21st inst in the attack on Fort Powhattan, were shot to death in Petersburg at a place called the "Gallows" designated for the execution of condemned criminals.

Five other prisoners have been captured from this Division, since it has been in occupation of points upon the James River of whose fate nothing is known at these Head Quarters.

I respectfully request that investigation may be had, to ascertain if the above mentioned report is true, and to determine what disposition has been made, of the other five prisoners alluded to.

I also request that Private Katon of the 24th Va. Regt, who was captured on the 18th inst, and all the prisoners captured from Genl Fitz Hugh Lee, at Wilson's Wharf on the 24th inst, be held for execution, in retaliation for the murder of the soldiers of the 22nd Regt, and of any other soldiers of this Division, who have met with a like fate, if the above report is known to be true.

I am General
Very Respectfully
Your Obt Servt
Edw W Hinks.
Brig Genl Commanding.

Hd. Qrs 54 Regt Mass Vols
Morris Id. S.C Nov. 23rd 1863

To His Excellency John A Andrew. Governor of Massachusetts
Governor.

Copies of

Your address, delivered to the Legislature of Massachusetts Nov. 11. 1863 have been received in this regiment. Such parts of it as recommend the General Court to authorize the payment to the enlisted men of the 54th Mass. Vols. of that portion of the lawful monthly pay of United States Volunteers which has been or may be refused them by the Paymaster of the United States, are received unfavorably by the enlisted men of this Regiment. They were enlisted and mustered into the Service of the United States with the understanding that they would be treated in all respects as other soldiers from Massachusetts. They will refuse to accept any money from the United States until the United States is willing to pay them according to the terms of their enlistment. They feel that by accepting a portion from the of their just dues from Massachusetts and a portion from the United States, they would be acknowledging a right on the part of the United States to draw a distinction between them and other soldiers from Massachusetts, and in so doing they would compromise their self respect. They enlisted because men were called for, and because the Government signified its willingness to accept them as such not because of the money offered them. They would rather work and fight until they are mustered out of the Service, without any pay, than accept from the Government less than it gives to other soldiers from Massachusetts, and by so accepting acknowledge that because they have African blood in their veins, they are less men, than those who have saxon.

Thanking you in behalf of the men, for the kind spirit you have always manifested in your efforts to establish their just rights

I remain
Very Respectfully.
Your Obdt. Svt.
(Sgd) E. N. Hallowell
Col. Comdg. 54 Mass

Document 18. Letter to governor of Massachusetts about equal pay for black troops, November 23, 1863. [National Archives]

New Orleans March 11/63

To General Banks

Dear Sir As A Part of the Militia of the State We the Undersigned free colored Men of the city of New Orleans wishing to organize the fifth 5th Regiment Louisiana Native Guards Appeals to you through this Medium to grant us the Privilege to Recruit Said Regiment with Captn B. M. Pratt of the 110th New york Regment as our choice for Colonel Our Great Desire is to strike A Blow for the Union therefore we are both willing and Ready to forsake our wives and Children And Risk the fortunes of War although Something New to us we are in hopes that the task Will Prove No harder to us than it was for our fathers in 1812 & 1815 we begs Pardon General for Our Intrusion but we still Indulge the hopes that Our Prayers May Meet With your favor with the Greatest Respects General we begs leave to be your humble Servent Please address John B. Bernabé In Care of Major G. K. Giddings Your Humble Servent

John B. Bernabé

Document 19. Letter to General Banks from free colored men of the city of New Orleans, March 11, 1863. [National Archives]

Balt Nov 7th

L Thomas Adgt Gen

Dear Sir

You will please
inform of the whereabuts of my
three sons not haveing heard
from them for a long time and
Since reported killed any
information Concerning them
Will be most thankfully received
by thair poor old Father
they are Named Peter Cook
Joseph Cook Joshua Cook
Compay E 30th Regt US CT
please adres Peter
Cook 558 West Baltimore Street
Balt Md

Philad.a February 8th 1865

To
The Secretary of War
Honl E. M. Stanton
W. D. Washington

Honl Sir

I am in great trouble of mind about my husband it is reported that he is dead he has been gone over a year and I have not hear from him his name is Samuel or Sandy Brown Co. C. 25th regiment U. S. Colored troops Penn he went with his brother and five Cousins to list they are all in same Co, and regiment none of them have been heard from only reports that they were dead which causes their wifes great grief. You will be doing charity by letting us know there whereabouts if alive so that we may write to them. Their names are Samuel or Sandy Brown Co. C. 25th regt Daniel Brown. Asa Miller. Daniel Horsey. George Horsey. Samuel Horsey George H. Washington they all belong to Same Co. and regiment, other side

We have not received a cent from them since they left we are all bad off it would do us a great favor if you would give the information as soon as your time will permit I am your obedient servant

Sarah Brown
Care of Peter Kelly
No 511 South 6th Street

Alexandria Va June the 11th

To the President of these U S S of Act

I a poor Offant have taken it upon myself to address these lines to you praying & beging you to look upon me & mine in Compashion & Grant me my patition & My prayer in the name & Strength of Jesus I come the Precious Saviour of the World Oh Honoured Sir Jesus died for you & every one Give Oh Give me my husband free discharge from the army I am in delicate health & cant get along without him & he has had no pay for 4 months he is Respected sir the only friend that I have in the world if I had Silver & Gold I would give all that I posesed but I have none but I have Jesus the Immaculate Lamb of God without spot or Blemish & I have maid My acquaintance

Document 22a. Letter to the President from Mrs. Stevens, June 11, 1865. [National Archives]

with him in these traits of his most noble
Character he is my only dearest Gracious
Tender Loving constant Compasionate
Omnipotent Omnepresent Simpothetic
Indulging Encouraging Coutious Conscious
Concuring Magnificient Expedicious Jesus
in these traits I have & do find him to be
perfection my Buckler & my Shield & my
Strong hold in the moment of need my poor
Husband was wounded last fall he had a
bullet through his right side & a slight
wound on his left Sholder he writes thus
I shall not be able to stand it much longer
my hip & Side is worst I shall have to give
up I am a dress maker Honered & Respected
Sir I have so many bitter things to go
through & being a very neat workman it puts
me on board of the slow train & sometimes
I am nearly starved before I can Acomplish
a piece of work Oh will you please favour me
by writing immediately to his Regiment in
North Carolina near Goldsborow for his

Document 22b. Letter to the President from Mrs. Stevens, June 11, 1865. [National Archives] discharge it will be attended to without delay from you & Kind Sir I unworthy I will agonise groan & pray to Jehoviah our Heavenly Father through his dear Son our Mediator for you & youre families prosperity & youre support in the Government I know that he sets in heaven & Answers prayor adress to Genl Blackman or Col Vanellen Commanding the Regt 3d Brigade 3 Division & 10 Army Corps Col Troops (My husband is a Sargent & his name is Joseph P Stevens I am in this dreary wide world all alone Oh give me give me my poor dear husband & I will be glad to fast & pray a day for you Kind Friend of Humanity & Justice & May God in his Infinite Mercy & Goodness bless & prosper you in Light knowledge wisdom & understanding the author of all things & keep you untill the end & rest youre soul in the haven of Sweet Repose & if a poor humble Womans prayors would be deemed a little help I am at youre Service at any time

Document 22c. Letter to the President from Mrs. Stevens, June 11, 1865. [National Archives]

S. 2040. June /65,

if at midnight—a line directed to Leouveture
Hospital will meet & immediate response.
if I am not asking two much & I have
found favour in your eys please send
me one line shed a ref of temporal joy
across my pathway I am depending on him
for Support—

Your Humble Subject
at your Service
Mr Stevens

P.S. ay the C. I.

Document 22d. Letter to the President from Mrs. Stevens, June 11, 1865. [National Archives]

New York, May the 24th 1865.

To the Hon. E. Mc Stanton, Secretary of War

I take the liberty to address myself to Your Honor, stating that my brother Samuel Peterson, coloured, has been drafted and served in Comp. H.C. Eight U.S. Regt. Infantry since 1863. He was wounded and taken prisoner at the battle of Mc Allister Florida, and was send from there to Andersonville as a prisoner, where he was kept from that time until the fourth of March last. He reached the Union lines on the 15th of March as a paroled prisoner and reached his home at Perth Amboy N. Jersey on the 18th last. All his expenses did fall upon me, being a servant myself. I have been employed for more than 12 years in the service of Mr U. A. Murdock President of the Continental Bank N.Y. which gentleman advised me to address Your Honor direct. I was obliged to hire a nurse for 58 days at the rate of $1.50 and board. The doctor's bill will be very heavy on me. So I do not know what to do to help myself

Several leading merchants in this city, besides Mr. Murdock my employer and Colonel Cannon assure me that they are confident Your Honor will do Something in my behalf. In the last place I suggest that my brother, Samuel Peterson has never received more than two months pay Since he entered the Service of the United States.

Respectfully

Your Obedient Servant

Peter Peterson.

313 fifth avenue N.Y.

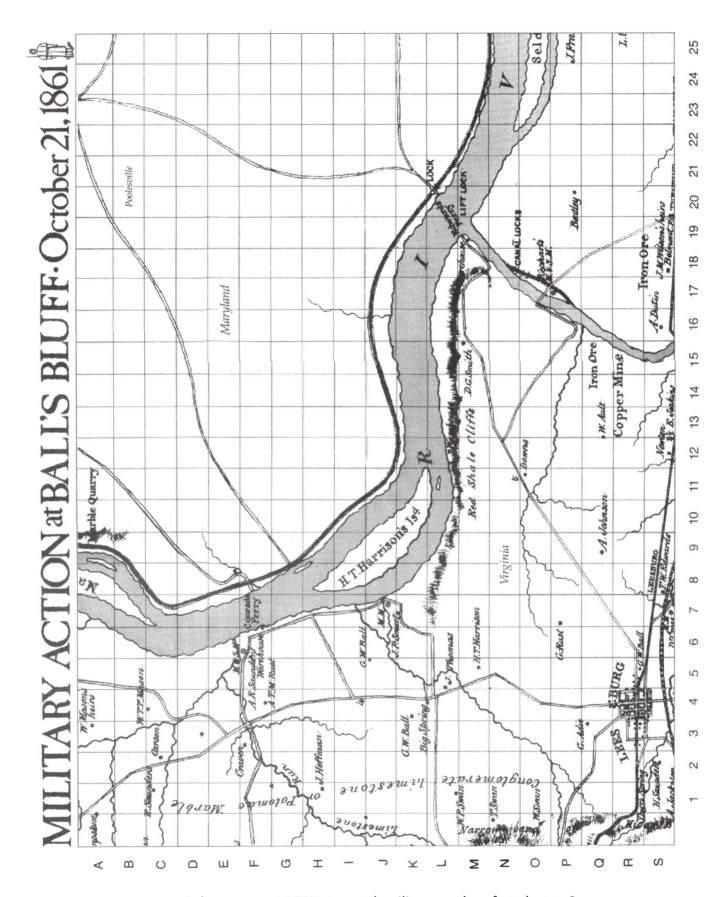

Enlarge map at 170% to match military markers from lesson 3

Document 24. Map, "Ball's Bluff, Loudoun County, Va., 1861." [National Archives]

Head-Quarters, Army of the Potomac,

Washington, November 1st 1861.

The Honorable Secretary of War

Sir

I have the honor to forward herewith Brig Gen Stone's report of the engagement near Leesburg on the 21st ult. I also transmit a copy of the telegram sent by me to Gen Stone on the 20th, being the same mentioned in the beginning of his report as the basis of his movements. I also enclose a copy of his telegram in reply on same date. My telegram did not contemplate the making an attack upon the enemy or the crossing of the river in force by any portion of Gen Stone's command, and not anticipating such movement I had upon the 20th directed Maj Gen McCall to return with his division on the morning of the 21st from Draineville to the camp from which he had advanced, provided the reconnoissances entrusted to him should have been then completed. Being advised by telegrams from Gen Stone received during the day and evening of the 21st of the crossing of the river the fall of Col Baker, the check sustained by our troops and that nearly all his (Stone's) force had crossed ~~was nearly of~~ the river, I sent to him at Edwards Ferry the following telegram at 10.30 P.M.; "Intrench yourself on the Virginia side and await reinforcements if necessary. I immediately telegraphed Maj Gen Banks to proceed with the three brigades of his division to the support of Gen Stone and advising ~~him~~ the latter that he would be thus supported, I directed him to hold his position at all hazards: On the 22d I went personally to the scene of operations and after ascertaining that the enemy were strengthening themselves at Leesburg and that our means of crossing and recrossing were very insufficient I withdrew our forces from the Virginia side.

I am sir very respectfully
your obdt. svt.

Geo B McClellan
Maj Genl Comdg USA

Poolesville Dec 2d

Lt Col Hardie
        A.D.C

                Stated concisely, the narration
would be this —

        Genl Stone directed Col Baker to
go to the right and in his discretion to
recall the troops then over the river or cross
more force — Col Baker made up his
mind & declared it before he reached
the crossing place; to cross with his
whole force —

        Genl Stone directed five companies
to be thrown into a strong mill on the
right of Ball's Bluff; Genl Col. Baker
allowed these companies to be diverted
to the front —

        Genl Stone sent cavalry scouts
to be thrown out in advance of the
infantry on the right — Col Baker
allowed this cavalry to return, without scouting & did
not replace it although he had
plenty at his disposition —

        Genl Stone Colonel Baker assumed
command on the right about 10 a.m.
but never sent an order or messenger
to the advanced infantry until it
was driven pressed back to the Bluff
about 2¼ P.M. —

        Col Baker spent more than

Document 26a. Letter from Charles P. Stone to Col. Hardie, December 2, 1861. [National Archives]

than an hour in personally superintending the lifting of a boat from the canal to the river when a junior officer or sergeant would have done as well, the meantime neglecting to give orders visit or to the advanced force in the ~~force~~ face of the enemy —

No order of passage was arranged for the boats, no guards were established at the landings — no boats crews detailed —

Lastly the troops were so arranged on the field as to expose ~~all their~~ them all, to fire ~~liver~~ while but few could fire on the enemy — His troops occupied all the cleared ground in the neighbourhood, while the enemy had the woods and the commanding wooded height which last he might easily have occupied before the enemy came up —

The written narrative will be sent tomorrow unless as today important duties prevent its being finished —

C. P. Stone

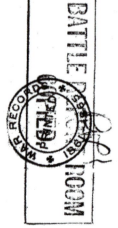

Document 26b. Letter from Charles P. Stone to Col. Hardie, December 2, 1861. [National Archives]

Col. E. D. Townsend
                    Sir

                    At the request of the relative
and many friends of Col. Baker, I have the honor
to submit a statement of the facts of the
engagement on last Monday the 21st inst, fought opposite
Harrison Island on the Virginia Shore.
In obedience to an order of Genl. Stone, the first
battalion of the California Regt. Baker's brigade,
under the command of Lieut. Col. Wistar, left Camp
Observation near the mouth of the Monocacy, at four
A.M. Monday, and reached Conrads ferry at
Sunrise. The battalion stacked arms, and I
proceeded to Edwards ferry distant five miles,
and reported to Genl. Stone for Orders, Lieut Howe
of the 15th Mass. arrived there at the Same time,
and reported that he had crossed the river at
Harrisons Island during the night and with some
others of his Regt. had Scouted the Country in the
direction of Leesburgh and found no enemy,
Genl. Stone then thereupon directed me to return to
Lieut. Col. Wistar with an order for the battalion
to stand fast until perchance he should hear
heavy firing in front, and in that event to Cross
to the Virginia Shore at Harrison Island;
At this time the summit of the Bluff opposite
the Island, on the Virginia Side, Was occupied by
Six Companies of the fifteenth Mass. Col Devans;
and a detatchment of the twentieth Mass. Col
Lee, And I was informed that two Companies
of the Tamany Regt. were there with them; also two small
howitzers of the R.I. battalion on the Island,
These forces having crossed during the night
preceeding and On my return to Col. Wistar,
irregular firing of musketry was heard from the

bluff; opposite the Island. Shortly afterwards Col Baker arrived with the other Officers of his Staff, and in a little while Genl Stone dispatched to him from Edwards ferry, an Order in writing, that in the event of heavy firing in direction of Harrisons Island, he should advance the California Regt, or retire the Union forces from the Virginia side of the river at his discretion; and to assume the Command on reaching the Virginia side. Col Baker immediately sent an order for three Regts. and a Squadron of Cavalry from his brigade, and for Col Coggswell, and the rest of his Tamany Regt.

Proceeding to the crossing at Harrisons Island, we found the means of transportation to consist of two flat boats of the capacity of twenty five to forty men, and a small skiff which would carry but three or four men. The river was swollen and Current rapid, and there was much labor and delay in making use of the boats. Another flat boat was found in the Canal one mile distant, and being towed down to the Crossing, was with much difficulty got into the Potomac. Col Baker immediately crossed with me and as many men as could be got into the boats, to the Island, and reaching the opposite side of the Island, found one flat boat, and a small Metalic boat. He crossed to the Virginia Shore without delay, with Adj. Genl. Harvey, Sending me back with an Order for Col Coggswell to bring over the Artillery. It was now two Oclock P.M. and Col Coggswell coming over from the Maryland side with two pieces of Artillery, horses & men, we carried with us the two howitzers of the R.I. Battery and crossed to the Virginia Side.

The bank is of Miry Clay, and the heights almost

precipitous, with fallen trees and rocks, making it very difficult to get up the Artillery. Arriving by circuitous route on the Summit, we found an open field of six Acres, covered with wild grass Scrub Oak and locust trees, and forming a Segment of a Circle, the arc of which, was surrounded with trees. Col Baker apprised Col Devin that he had been placed in command, and learned that the Maj. fifteenth. After having advanced for a mile in the direction of Leesburgh had been attacked, and ~~had~~ fallen back to the position which they then occupied just in the edge of the woods, on the right The other forces were lying under the brow of the hill, and with the exception of an occasional rifle Shot, all was quiet and no sight of an Enemy. The two howitzers and one piece of Artillery were drawn by the men out into the open field, pointing to the woods in front; the Artillery horses not being brought up ~~and of no~~ the steep. ~~Service~~. After a quarter of an hour had passed, the enemy making no Sign, two Cos of the California battalion, A & D. were sent out from the left as Skirmishers through the wood. They had advanced but a few rods, when with a Yell a tremendous volley of rifle shot from the concealed Enemy drove them back; and from that ~~time~~ moment up to the fall of Col Baker, there was no cessation of heavy firing from the Enemy in the woods. The reinforcements from the Island came up very slowly and it was Evident to all, that unless aid in force reached us from the left, we should be driven into the river, as the increasing Yells and firing of the enemy indicated their larger number and nearer approach.
The two howitzers were of no Service, and the twelve pounder ~~was but occasionally fired, being~~

being Manned by Col Baker, Lieut Col Wistar, Adj Genl Harvey, Capt Bieral and a few privates of his Co. G. The piece was fired not more than five or six times; and excepting the last time, with doubtful effect, As the Enemy was at no time visible, We simply fired at the woods. Col Baker was at all times in the open field, walking in front of the men lying on the ground, exibiting the greatest coolness and courage. The fire of the enemy was constant, and bullets fell like hail Stones, but it was evident that the enemy was firing into the open field without direct aim. Col. Baker fell about five Oclock; He was Standing near the left of the wood, and it is believed he was Shot with a Cavalry revolver by a private of the enemy, Who, after Col Baker fell, crawled on his hands and knees to the body, and was attempting to take his sword, When Capt Bieral with ten of his men rushed up and shot him through the head, and rescued the body; At the time Col Baker was shot, he was looking at a mounted Officer, who rode down a few rods into the field, from the woods, who being shot at by one of our men, returned to the woods, and appeared to be falling from his horse, Col Baker turning about, said, "see he falls" and immediately fell, receiving four balls each of which would be fatal, I had but a moment before, Standing by his side, been ordered by Col. Baker to go with all possible dispatch to Genl Stone for reinforcements on the left, as there was no transportation across the river for the wants of the hour, There was some confusion on the field, and the officers of the Cos of the fifteenth Mass. Regt. ordered their men to retreat.

The Enemy then for the first time came out of the Wood at double quick, and receiving a double charge of grape shot from the twelve pounder and broke in disorder and returned to the woods. There were but few of the federal forces now on the field, they having returned to the river side, down the Steep, but finding no means of escape, Some two hundred charged up the hill and poured in a Volley, the enemy at this time occupying the field. It was getting dark and some one tied a white hdkf. to a Sword and went forward. Many were taken prisoners at the moment and some fled into the woods on either side, and many others ran down to the Crossing. I got the body of Col Baker on the flat boat, at this time partly filled with water, and The dead & wounded, and safely reached the Island, Throwing away their arms, the men Swam the river, the enemy firing upon them from the hights, The boat returning to the Virginia Side was Overcrowded and being leaky, Sank in the middle of the river, many drowned at that time. Lieut Col Wistar an hour before, having received four Shots in various parts of his body, had been carried from the field. And Col Coggswell being wounded in the arm, there was no Officer in Command. Adj. Genl. Harvey had a Shot in his cheek, but remained on the field and was taken prisoner. Col Devens safely reached the Shore, but I can give no information concerning Col Lee, he with Col Coggswell are probably prisoners. When Col Coggswell crossed the river, he brought a second order in writing with him from Genl Stone, to the Effect that Col Baker should lose no time in, if he could advancing in the direction

of Leesburg, & that he might count upon
Meeting the enemy in force of about four
thousand,

These orders I found in Genl Bakers hat after
he had fallen, Stained with his blood. During the
engagement our forces to the number of five
thousand, with many pieces of Artillery
were in plain view on the Maryland side, but
having no means of transportation, were of
no Service.

The position occupied by our forces was but
a few rods from the river side, and there were
no houses or roads in view. I have no means
of Stating acuratily the Number of our loss, but
that of the California battalion, which is about
two three hundred, Col Baker and Sixty out
# of Six hundred and Eighty nine. Col Baker and
all the officers were on foot throughout the en-
-gagement, leaving their horses tied to the trees
and they all fell into the hands of the Enemy.
There was an ineffectual effort to throw the
twelve pounder and howitzers down the Steep into the river,
and the howitzers were also thrown down the
hill, but being obstructed by fallen trees, they
did not reach the water, and the next day
were drawn by the enemy upon the hill. A first
Lieut of the 8th Regt Virginia named J. wax Berry infantry, by mistake
rode into our lines having been left behind by
his Co. and was taken prisoner in the early part of
the engagement & sent to our camp. He states that
the rebels are abundantly supplied with arms,
ammunition & rations, but are sadly in want of
clothing. A few privates also fell into our hands, but not being
able to carry them away, they escaped from us, The
depth of the river at the crossing ranges from

three to ten feet, and the width of the first crossing is about one hundred yards, and of the second, about ~~about~~ sixty yards, it maybe more. There was no regularity or order in the movement of the boats.

I have the honor to be
Your obedient servant

Capt. Francis G. Young
of Genl Bakers Staff

Head Quarters 7" Brigade
Leesburg Va,
October 31" 1861

Colonel —

I beg leave to submit the following report of the action of the troops of the 7" Brigade in the Battle of the 21st and 22nd Instant with the Enemy at Leesburg Va.

On Saturday night, the 19th Instant, about 7 o'clock P.M., the Enemy commenced a heavy Cannonading from three batteries, One playing on my Entrenchment (Known as Fort Evans), One on the Leesburg Turnpike, And one on Edwards' Ferry. Heavy firing was also heard in the direction of Dranesville —

At 12 o'clock at night, I ordered my Entire Brigade to the Burnt Bridge on the Turnpike. The Enemy had been reported as approaching from Dranesville in large force. Taking a strong position on the north side of Goose Creek, I awaited his Approach — Reconnoitering the Turnpike on Sunday morning, the Courier of Genl. McCall was Captured, bearing despatches to Genl. Meade, to Examine the roads leading to Leesburg — From this prisoner I learned the position of the Enemy near Dranesville — During Sunday the Enemy Kept a deliberate fire, without any effect.

Early on Monday morning, the 21st Instant, I heard the firing of my picketts at Big Spring, who had discovered that, at an unguarded point, the Enemy had effected a crossing in force of five Companies, and were advancing on Leesburg. Capt. Duff, of the 17 Reg.t immediately attacked him, driving him back with several killed and wounded.

On observing the movements of the Enemy from Fort Evans, at six o'clock A.M., I found he had effected a crossing both at Edwards' Ferry and Balls Bluff and I made preparations to meet him in both positions, And immediately ordered four Companies Infantry (Two of the 18" one of the 17th and one of the 13th) and a Cavalry force to relieve Capt. Duff; the whole force under the immediate Command of Lt. Col. W. H. Jenifer, who was directed to hold his position till the Enemy made further demonstration of his design of attack. This force soon became warmly— Engaged with the Enemy and drove them back for some distance in the woods.

At about 10 o'clock I became convinced that the main point of attack would be at Ball's Bluff, And ordered Col Hunton with his Regiment, the 8th Va. Vols, to repair immediately to the support of Col Jenifer. I directed Col Hunton to form line of battle immediately in the rear of Col Jenifer's Command and to drive the Enemy to the river, that I would support his right with Artillery — About twenty minutes past 12 O'clock Meridian, Col. Hunton united his Command with that of Col. Jenifer, And both Commands soon became hotly Engaged with the Enemy in their strong position in the woods.   Watching, carefully, the action I saw the Enemy were constantly being reinforced, and at halfpast Two o'clock, P.M., ordered Col. Burt to march his Regiment, the 18" Miss., and attack the left flank of the Enemy, while Col. Hunton and Jenifer attacked him in front. On arriving at his position Col Burt was received with a tremendous fire from the Enemy concealed in a Ravine, and was compelled to divide his Regiment to stop the flank movement of the Enemy.

At this time, about Three o'clock, finding the Enemy were in large force, I ordered Col Featherston with his Regiment, the 17" Miss. to repair, at Double Quick, to the support of Col. Burt, where he arrived in twenty minutes, and the Action became general along my whole line, and was very hot and brisk for more than two hours, the Enemy keeping up a constant fire with his batteries on both sides of the river.

At about six o'clock, P.M. I saw that my Command had driven the Enemy near the banks of the Potomac; I ordered my Entire force to charge and to drive him into the river. The charge was immediately made by the Whole Command and the forces of the Enemy were completely routed, and cried out for quarter along his whole line.

In this charge the Enemy were driven back at the point of the bayonet and many killed and

4

wounded by this formidable weapon — In the precipitate retreat of the enemy on the bluffs of the river many of his troops rushed into the water and were drowned, while many others, in overloading the boats, sunk them, and shared the same fate.

The rout now, about Seven O'clock, became Complete, and the Enemy Commenced throwing his arms into the river.

During this Action I held Col. Wm Barksdale with Nine Companies of his Regiment, the 13" Miss., And Six pieces of Artillery as a reserve, as well as to keep up a demonstration against the force of the Enemy at Edwards' Ferry.

At Eight o'clock P.M. the Enemy Sur= rendered his forces at Ball's Bluff— and the prisoners were marched to Leesburg—

I then ordered my Brigade, (with the Exception of the 13" Reg.t Miss., who remained in front of Edwards' Ferry), to retire to the Town of Leesburg and rest for the night—

8

The Engagement on our side was fought entirely with the musket, The Artillery was in position to do effective service should the enemy have advanced from their Cover.

The Enemy were Armed with the minie musket, the Belgian gun, and Springfield musket; a Telescopic Target rifle was also among the Arms found.

In closing my report I would Call the attention of the General Commanding to the heroism and gallantry displayed by the officers and Men of the 7th Brigade in the Actions of the 21st and 22d of October. The promptness with which every Com= mander obeyed, and the spirit with with which their men executed my orders to attack the enemy in much superior force and in a position where he had great Advantages, Entitles them to the thanks of the Southern Confederacy. ⸺ Without food or rest for more than Twelve hours previous to the Commence= ment of the battle, they drove an enemy, four times their number, from the soil of Virginia, Killing and taking prisoners a greater number than our whole force engaged ⸺ To witness the patience

9.

Enthusiasm and devotion of the troops to our cause during an action of Thirteen hours, excited my warmest admiration.

As My Entire Brigade exceeded my most sanguine expectations, in their intrepidity and endurance, I am unable to individualize any particular Command, as the tenacity with which

Document 28e. Excerpt from letter from N. G. Evans, October 31, 1861. [National Archives]

each regiment held their positions was equaled only by their undaunted courage and firm determination to Conquer.

Very Respectfully
Your Obt Ser
NG Evans
Brig Genl,
Comdg 7th Brigade

To

Lt Col Thos Jordan
Asst Adjt Genl
1st Corps Army Potomac
Near Centreville

No. 2.

Reports of Colonel Edward W. Hinks, 19th Mass Vols.

Head quarters 19th Mass Vols
Camp Benton
near Poolesville Md Oct 23rd .61.

Brig Genl F W Lander
            Sir

            Learning that a column of our
troops was crossing the Potomac, on the 21st inst,
at a point near the centre of Harrison's Island,
in which the companies of my regiment, stationed
as pickets upon the river, had been ordered
to join by Genl Baker, I hastened thither
in anticipation of orders from Genl Stone.

            I arrived there about half past one
o'clock P M, and found among the troops,
at the point of crossing, great confusion,
no competent officer seeming to have been
left in charge of the transportation, and
the progress made in embarking was very
slow. I at once took charge at this
point, caused a line to be stretched across

Document 29a. Excerpt from letter to Brigadier General Lauder
from Edward W. Hinks, October 23, 1861. [National Archives]

the power by which to propel the boats and forwarded troops in the following order, to wit; Part of California regiment not already crossed, the Rhode Island and New York batteries, the 42 New York (Tammany) regiment and the 19th Massachussetts.

I cannot close this report, with justice to our troops, who fought valiantly, without commenting upon the causes which led to their defeat and complete rout.

The means of transportation, for advance in support or for a retreat were criminally deficient, especially when we consider the facility for creating proper means for such purposes at our disposal.

The place for landing upon the Virginia shore was most unfortunately selected, being at a point where the shore rose with great abruptness for a distance of some one hundred and fifty yards, at an angle in many places of at least twenty five degrees, and was studded with trees, being entirely impassable to Artillery or Infantry in line. At the summit the surface is undulating, where the enemy were placed in force, out of view, and cut down our troops with a murderous fire, which we could not return with any effect. The entire Island was also commanded by the enemy's Artillery and rifles. In fact no more unfortunate position could have been forced upon us by the enemy for making an attack. much less selected by ourselves. Within a half mile upon either side of the point selected a landing could have been effected where we could have been placed upon equal terms with the enemy, if it was necessary to effect a landing from the Island. My judgment however cannot approve of that policy which multiplies the number of river crossings without any conpursuation in securing commanding positions thereby

Respectfully submitted
Edward W. Hinks
Col. 19th Mass Vols
Comdg Brigade

Note† The fact that the remaining fragment of the Tammany Regiment had left the Island without orders, was construed by the Confederate Commandant as a violation of the stipulation that "no movement of troops should be made from the Island to the Maryland shore until the burying party was employed"

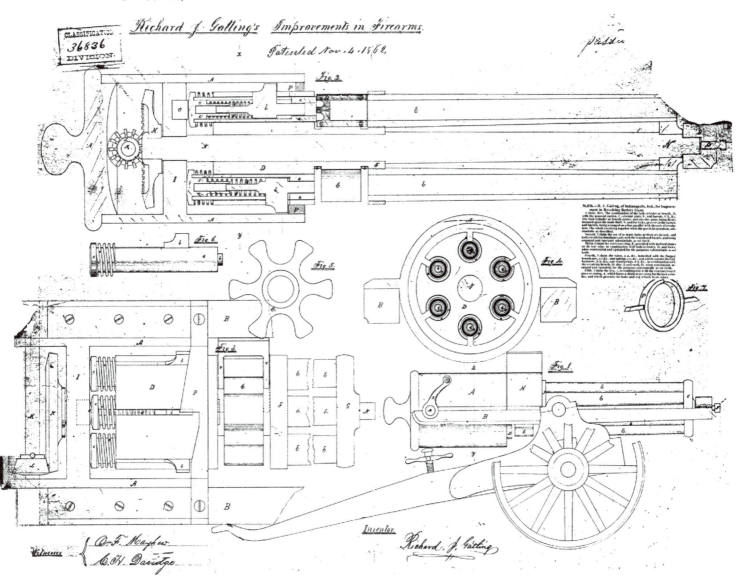

Document 30. Patent drawing, R. J. Gatling's "Revolving Battery"
(Gun), patented November 4, 1862. [National Archives]

Ganster's

Percussion Hand Grenade.

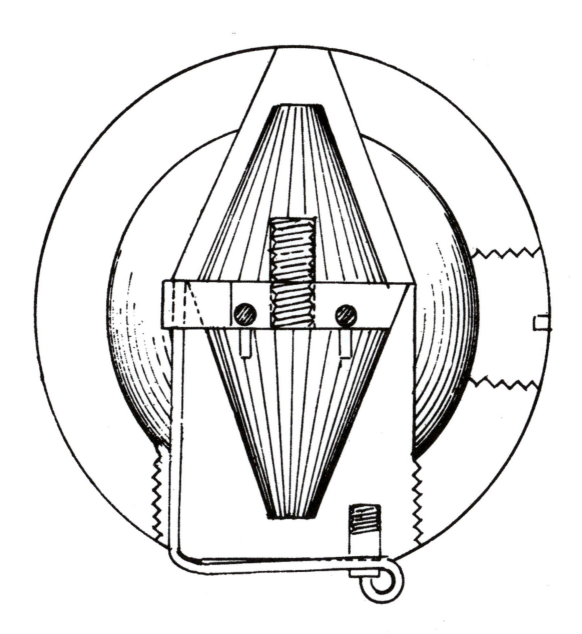

Document 31. Drawing of "Ganster's Percussion
Hand Grenade," October 24, 1864. [National Archives]

Mr. Ganster's Percussion Hand Grenade

Navy Ordnance Yard
Washington City, October 24th 1864.

Commander H. A. Wise
    Chief of Bureau of Ordnance.
    Sir :—

    In accordance with Bureau order of October 1st, I have made trial in presence of the Inventor of the Percussion hand Grenade presented by Mr George P. Ganster.

    It consists of Spherical ball $2\frac{3}{4}$ in. in diameter with a hole for the insertion of the percussion apparatus and one for filling it stopped by a brass screw plug. Weight 2 lbs.

    The percussion apparatus consist of two cones kept apart by a spiral spring: On the base of one of them the heads of three of the common "parlor" matches are stuck in holes.

    To prevent accidental concussion, a lever is so arranged as to secure one of the cones so that contact cannot take place until it is unlocked.

    A drawing is attached showing the internal arrangement more fully.

    Eight were thrown by the inventor, to a mean distance of 25 yards all exploding on impact. The pieces were thrown in every direction with great force, — pieces striking the bomb proof in which the inventor and myself were sheltered with force sufficient to inflict a dangerous if not mortal wound One was thrown several times without being unlocked in order to prove their safety in transport.

    Unlocked and let fall from a height of five feet thus explode.

    In my opinion such projectiles are not suited to the requirements of the Naval Service.

    To use the words of a recent French writer —

    "Grenades are detestable projectiles, which are more likely to damage "those who use them than those against whom they are employed"
    "They are only of service when they can be used by persons —

completely under cover against others entirely exposed" In which opinion I fully concur.

Very respectfully
Your Obt Servant
William N. Jeffers
Inspector of Ordnance, in charge of
Experimental Department~

Hyde's War Rockets.

Ordnance Yard, Novemb. 18th 1862.

Captain I. A. Dahlgren
　　　Chief of Bureau of Ordnance.
　　Sir:

In relation to the War Rockets, presented by Mr. Hyde. I have to report, as follows.

In the head of this rocket was a shell designed to explode by a time fuze.

The perforations of this rocket to obtain a rotary motion were at is centre of gravity.

On the 15th inst. one was fired with the following result.
His Excellency, A. Lincoln, President of the United States.
Hon. Wm H. Seward, Secretary of State.
Hon. S. P. Chase, Secretary of Treasury, and
Captain I. A. Dahlgren. Chief of Bureau of Ordnance were present.

Officer in Charge, Lieut. Comdr. Wm Mitchell.
Weight and dimensions of rocket. not taken.
Rocket stand used _ a perforated iron Cylinder
　　　Elevation 20° by quadrant
Rocket burst in the stand _ fired with a percussion cap.

On the 17th inst. another was fired from an open wooden trough.

Lieut. Comdr. Wm Mitchell, in charge.
Weight of Rocket　　　17 lbs 1
Length of 　"　　　　　2. 3 in
Diameter of 　"　　　　3. in
Fired with quick match _____

"Over."

Document 33a. Letter to Captain Dahlgren from William Mitchell, November 18, 1862. [National Archives]

Rocket left the stand and at a short distance from, ascended into the air, whirling at the same time, took a direction nearly at right angles to the line of fire, and fell upon the roof of the Blacksmith Shop, and thence to the ground.

It was considered dangerous to continue the experiment by the inventor, and consequently suspended it.

Very respectfully,
Wm Mitchell
Lieut. Comdr.
U.S.N.

Index of patents issued from the United States Patent Office from 1790 to 1873, inclusive—Continued.

Invention.	Inventor.	Residence.	Date.	No.
Animal-trap	S. S. Rain	Lowville, N. Y	July 7, 1868	79, 686
Animal-trap	N. Rasmussen	Chicago, Ill	Oct. 3, 1871	119, 645
Animal-trap	S. Reed	Whitestown, Pa	Jan. 14, 1868	73, 384
Animal-trap	W. N. Reed	Washington, D. C	Sept. 21, 1869	94, 975
Animal-trap	E. Reichard	Washington, Mo	Oct. 13, 1868	83, 094
Animal-trap	J. H. Reisinger	Vinton, Ohio	May 5, 1868	77, 657
Animal-trap	F. Reuthe	Hartford, Conn	May 12, 1857	17, 297
Animal-trap	F. Reuthe	Hartford, Conn	Aug. 24, 1858	21, 302
Animal-trap	J. H. Richardson	Westport, Mo	Sept. 13, 1870	107, 292
Animal-trap	T. L. Rivers	Saint Louis, Mo	May 19, 1868	78, 015
Animal-trap	J. Rollins	Kingston, Tenn	Mar. 26, 1872	124, 976
Animal-trap	B. F. Sanford	Galesburgh, Ill	Dec. 5, 1865	51, 356
Animal-trap	J. Schroy	Fortville, Ind	Nov. 5, 1867	70, 624
Animal-trap	H. Seehausen	Memphis, Tenn	Jan. 25, 1870	99, 245
Animal-trap	T. Shailer	Haddam, Conn	May 10, 1844	3, 580
Animal-trap	J. Sherman	New Oxford, Pa	Sept. 1, 1868	81, 829
Animal-trap	T. Silliman	Three Rivers, Mich	Nov. 26, 1867	71, 543
Animal-trap	T. Silliman	Three Rivers, Mich	Apr. 27, 1869	89, 352
Animal-trap	R. Simpson	Port Jefferson, Ohio	Oct. 29, 1867	70, 370
Animal-trap	J. A. Sinclair	Woodsfield, Ohio	Feb. 18, 1868	74, 617
Animal-trap	G. Slusser	Hillsborough, Ohio	Aug. 14, 1860	29, 627
Animal-trap	B. C. Smith	Pekin, Ill	July 11, 1871	117, 005
Animal-trap	B. F. Smith	Philadelphia, Pa	Oct. 14, 1873	143, 727
Animal-trap	E. B. Smith	Marietta, Ohio	June 30, 1868	79, 506
Animal-trap	O. R. Smith	Elgin, Minn	Aug. 11, 1868	81, 023
Animal-trap	V. O. and J. R Spencer	Mansfield, Pa	Feb. 7, 1860	27, 080
Animal-trap	E. Sprague and G. C. Belt	Bridgeton, Ind	June 28, 1870	104, 896
Animal-trap	W. A. Stack	Hillsborough, Md	Nov. 10, 1868	84, 013
Animal-trap	W. L. Starr	Columbus, Ohio	Mar. 31, 1868	76, 289
Animal-trap	J. J. St. Ledger	Philadelphia, Pa	Mar. 30, 1869	88, 526
Animal-trap	A. Storm	Brooklyn, N. Y	Feb. 5, 1867	61, 889
Animal-trap	J. N. Stow and R. Loop	Camden, Ohio	Apr. 25, 1871	114, 002
Animal-trap	Z. Swope	Lancaster, Pa	Aug. 16, 1859	25, 224
Animal-trap	J. Teed	Tompkins, N. Y	Apr. 16, 1867	63, 961
Animal-trap	A. C. Thomas	Camp Charlotte, Ohio	Feb. 11, 1868	74, 256
Animal-trap	J. S. Thompson	Sycamore, Ill	Feb. 11, 1868	74, 451
Animal-trap	N. S. Thompson	Germantown, Ohio	Jan. 21, 1868	73, 475
Animal-trap	W. Tinsley	New York, N. Y	Feb. 7, 1860	27, 083
Animal-trap	R. Tompkins	Clarksville, Tenn	Nov. 23, 1869	97, 248
Animal-trap	J. Trainer	Rural Dale, Ohio	Oct. 22, 1867	70, 133
Animal-trap	J. Trainer	Vinton Station, Ohio	May 19, 1868	78, 029
Animal-trap	C. S. Trevitt	Washington, D. C	Oct. 22, 1867	70, 134
Animal-trap	R. M. Turner	Woodland, Mich	Sept. 7, 1858	21, 454
Animal-trap	J. L. Tusten	Winona, Miss	Nov. 9, 1869	96, 744
Animal-trap	T. B. Van Pelt	Westport, Mo	July 20, 1869	92, 911
Animal-trap	C. B. Veronee	Athens, Ga	Apr. 4, 1871	113, 371
Animal trap	G. S. Walker	Erie, Pa	Aug. 22, 1871	118, 309
Animal-trap	S. Ward	Richmond, Ill	Sept. 24, 1867	69, 279
Animal-trap	A. L. Waring	Coshocton, Ohio	Oct. 13, 1868	83, 011
Animal-trap	A. Warner	Cleveland, Ohio	Sept. 23, 1862	36, 543
Animal-trap	J. Westcott	Patchogue, N. Y	Oct. 15, 1867	69, 878
Animal-trap	L. Wetmore	Tioga County, Pa	July 12, 1859	24, 771
Animal-trap	J. Wheelock	San Francisco, Cal	Mar. 7, 1865	46, 741
Animal-trap	J. P. Wigal	Henderson, Ky	Jan. 14, 1868	73, 418
Animal-trap	H. Y. Wildey	Philadelphia, Pa	Oct. 2, 1860	30, 269
Animal-trap	J. M. Wilkinson	Bloomington, Tenn	Sept. 2, 1873	142, 362
Animal-trap	W. T. Williams	New York, N. Y	Feb. 19, 1861	31, 504
Animal-trap	J. P. Wilson	Frankfort, N. Y	Jan. 31, 1860	27, 017
Animal-trap	G. Wolf	Williamsport, Md	Apr. 24, 1866	54, 241
Animal-trap	J. J. Wood	North Manchester, Ind	Sept. 27, 1870	107, 844
Animal-trap	R. E. Wood	Santa Cruz, Cal	Nov. 29, 1870	109, 789
Animal-trap	W. J. Woodside	Zanesville, Ohio	Apr. 28, 1868	77, 341
Animal-trap	W. Wright	Philadelphia, Pa	June 19, 1860	28, 820
Animal-trap	H. D. Wrightson	Queenstown, Md	Mar. 7, 1871	112, 403
Animal-trap	C. Zaiser	Newark, N. J	Feb. 11, 1868	74, 264
Animal-trap adjustable platform	J. Thomas	West Chester, Pa	June 26, 1849	6, 554
Animal-trap and seed-safe combined	S. V. Greer	Rocky Hill Station, Ky	July 15, 1873	140, 773
Animal-trap, Construction of	M. H. Biddle	Mount Carmel, Ill	Oct. 5, 1858	21, 647
Animal-trap, Construction of	E. Hill	Cincinnati, Ohio	Oct. 5, 1858	21, 676
Animal-trap, Device for setting	I. Miller	Bryan, Ohio	Sept. 10, 1867	68, 776
Animal-trap, Manufacture of	C. Jillson	Worcester, Mass	Jan. 6, 1857	16, 353
Animal-trap, Self-setting	H. B. Myers	Schoolcraft, Mich	Feb. 14, 1865	46, 379
Animal-trap wheel	W. F. Collier	Worcester, Mass	June 13, 1871	115, 933
Animal-trap wheel	B. B. and J. R. Hill	Worcester, Mass	July 4, 1871	116, 592
Animals against flies, Lotion for protecting	J. Greene	Providence, R. I	Oct. 24, 1871	120, 191
Animals, Apparatus for relieving choked	G. Clump	Hamden, Conn	Apr. 21, 1868	76, 998
Animals, Apparatus for taming wild	P. R. Sanderson	Caledonia, N. Y	Dec. 10, 1867	71, 914
Animals, Brand for marking	H. Thompson	Hector, N. Y	Apr. 30, 1867	64, 263
Animals, Device for catching	W. L. Hopper	Monmouth, Ill	Aug. 27, 1867	68, 197
Animals, Device for catching and holding domestic	H. V. Van Etten	Auburn, N. Y	Dec. 29, 1868	85, 413
Animals from railways, Apparatus for removing	L. Montgilion	Elk Ridge Landing, Md	Feb. 13, 1849	6, 113
Animals from the heat of the sun, Mode of protecting	C. Elveena	New York, N. Y	Sept. 18, 1866	58, 081
Animals, Instrument for administering balls to	T. H. Bex	Syracuse, N. Y	June 17, 1873	139, 856
Animals, Slings for raising	F. Hohorst	New York, N. Y	Feb. 18, 1873	136, 059
Ankle-brace	J. S. Niswander	Oakland, Cal	Mar. 21, 1871	112, 952
Ankle-brace	S. B. Sherer	Aurora, Ill	Apr. 7, 1868	76, 353
Ankle-brace joint	E. E. Howe	Boston, Mass	Aug. 20, 1872	130, 639
Ankle or knee guard	H. A. Hall	Boston, Mass	May 12, 1868	77, 728
Ankle-supporter	R. Cunningham	Chicago, Ill	Mar. 20, 1866	53, 276
Ankle supporter and filler	S. Silberschmidt	Baltimore, Md	Oct. 7, 1873	143, 537
Ankles, Surgical apparatus for fractured or injured	G. W. Yerger	Philadelphia, Pa	Mar. 20, 1849	6, 214
Annealing and hardening metals, Process for	J. N. Lauth	Pittsburgh, Pa	Oct. 29, 1872	132, 675
Annealing and swaging castings, Method of	E. B. Wilson	Westminster, England	Sept. 17, 1861	33, 315
Annealing-apparatus	J. Worcester	Newport, Ky	Sept. 25, 1860	30, 174
Annealing-box	J. C. Lewis	Sharpsburgh, Pa	May 1, 1866	54, 376
Annealing car-wheels	A. L. Mowry	Cincinnati, Ohio	May 7, 1861	32, 252
Annealing cut-nails	J. McCarty	Reading, Pa	June 11, 1861	32, 525

Index of patents issued from the United States Patent Office from 1790 to 1873, inclusive—Continued.

Invention.	Inventor.	Residence.	Date.	No.
Arithmetical frame	H. K. Bugbee	New York, N. Y	July 12, 1864	43,545
Arithmetical frame	E. T. Curtis	Calumet, Mich	Aug. 26, 1873	142,151
Arithmetical sum setter	A. W. Price	Detroit, Mich	Apr. 23, 1872	126,123
Arithmometer	T. Hill	Waltham, Mass	Nov. 24, 1857	18,692
Arithmometer for adding	O. L. Castle	Upper Alton, Ill	Nov. 24, 1857	18,675
Arithmometer for addition	O. L. Castle	Upper Alton, Ill	Nov. 2, 1858	21,941
Ark, Safety	W. Hollins	Baltimore, Md	May 4, 1824	....
Arm and hand, Artificial	B. F. Palmer	Philadelphia, Pa	Jan. 11, 1859	22,576
Arm and hand, Artificial	T. Uren	New York, N. Y	Jan. 31, 1865	46,158
Arm and hand, Artificial	T. Uren	New York, N. Y	Jan. 31, 1865	46,159
Arm, Artificial	J. Condell	Morristown, N. Y	July 11, 1865	48,659
Arm, Artificial	E. Cotly	Washington, D. C	Oct. 27, 1863	40,397
Arm, Artificial	H. A. Kimball and A. J. Lawrence.	Philadelphia, Pa	May 23, 1865	47,835
Arm, Artificial	J. H. Koeller	New York, N. Y	July 19, 1864	43,590
Arm, Artificial	J. H. Koeller	New York, N. Y	Oct. 11, 1864	44,638
Arm, Artificial	D. W. Kolbe	Philadelphia, Pa	Nov. 15, 1864	45,052
Arm, Artificial	M. Lincoln	Malden, Mass	Aug. 11, 1863	39,487
Arm, Artificial	A. McOmber	Schenectady, N. Y	Jan. 1, 1867	60,921
Arm, Artificial	J. Peterson	Canoga, N. Y	Mar. 7, 1865	46,696
Arm, Artificial	E. Spellerberg	Philadelphia, Pa	Apr. 26, 1864	42,515
Arm, Artificial	E. Spellerberg	Philadelphia, Pa	Nov. 28, 1865	51,238
Arm, Artificial	I. Stoffel	Washington, D. C	Jan. 10, 1865	45,876
Arm, Artificial	I. Stoffel	Washington, D. C	Aug. 28, 1866	57,594
Arm. Artificial	T. Uren	New York, N. Y	May 30, 1865	48,002
Arm-chair, Folding	H. S. Golightly and C. S. Twitchell.	New Haven, Conn	June 28, 1864	43,366
Arm-chair, Folding	W. C. Goodwin	Hamden, Conn	Jan. 1, 1862	34,380
Arm-rest and paper-cutter, Combined	C. B. Dickinson	Brooklyn, N. Y	May 26, 1868	78,192
Arm-rest, Compositor's	C. L. Alexander	Washington, D. C	May 28, 1872	127,208
Arm-rest, Penman's	J. B. Withey	Lexington, Mich	May 26, 1868	78,250
Arm-support for keyed instrument	L. Buchbuger	Chicago, Ill	Nov. 29, 1870	109,582
Arms, Slinging	O. E. Woods	Philadelphia, Pa	May 15, 1866	54,807
Arms-supporter for riflemen	S. Kinman	Humboldt, Cal	Feb. 14, 1865	46,365
Arms-supporter, India-rubber	H. Greentree	Baltimore, Md	Dec. 12, 1871	121,868
Armillary sphere	H. Bryant	Hartford, Conn	Sept. 10, 1872	131,148
Armlet	A. S. Potter	Providence, R. I	Apr. 9, 1872	125,407
Arm-pit shield	W. E. Beames	New York, N. Y	Oct. 22, 1872	132,348
Arm-pit shield	J. Sibley	New York, N. Y	Sept. 16, 1873	142,875
Armor, Defensive	C. H. Hudson	Roxbury, Mass	Sept. 27, 1864	44,426
Armor for marine and other batteries, Defensive	J. B. Eads	Saint Louis, Mo	July 14, 1863	39,218
Armor for ship	T. Whitby	Lambeth, England	Sept. 3, 1867	68,474
Armor for ship, Defensive	M. L. Callender and N. W. Northrup.	New York and Greene, N. Y.	May 27, 1862	35,412
Armor for ships and other batteries, Defensive	C. W. S. Heaton	Belleville, Ill	Apr. 14, 1863	38,206
Armor for ships and other batteries, Defensive	R. H. Jewett	Mount Sterling, Ill	Feb. 17, 1863	37,695
Armor for ships and other batteries, Defensive	R. Montgomery	New York, N. Y	Feb. 10, 1863	37,633
Armor for ships and other batteries, Defensive	W. W. W. Wood	Philadelphia, Pa	Sept. 23, 1862	36,546
Armor for ships, batteries, &c., Defensive	G. B. Manley	Danville, Pa	Jan. 13, 1863	37,402
Armor for ships, Construction of the defensive	W. Rumbold	Saint Louis, Mo	July 15, 1862	35,895
Armor for ships, Metallic defensive	W. Ballard	New York, N. Y	June 24, 1862	35,665
Armor for water and land batteries, Defensive	J. L. Jones	Saint Louis, Mo	Apr. 15, 1862	35,001
Armor, Metallic defensive	B. B. Hotchkiss	Sharon, Conn	Aug. 12, 1862	36,152
Armor, Naval defensive	G. M. Mowbray	Titusville, Pa	Sept. 9, 1862	36,439
Armor plate, Defensive	E. Cox	Covington, Ky	May 27, 1862	35,364
Armor-plate, Defensive	M. Wappich	Sacramento, Cal	Mar. 3, 1863	37,836
Armor-plate for land or marine battery	F. P. Dimpfel	Philadelphia, Pa	Aug. 4, 1863	39,384
Armor-plate for marine or other batteries, Means of connecting metallic.	T. Shaw	Philadelphia, Pa	May 13, 1862	35,279
Armor-plate for ships and other batteries	B. T. Babbitt	New York, N. Y	Jan. 13, 1863	37,380
Armor-plate for vessels	J. F. Winslow	Troy, N. Y	May 27, 1862	35,407
Armor-plate, Ships'	H. H. Warden	New York, N. Y	Feb. 25, 1862	34,539
Armor-plates, Means of affixing defensive	E. Brady	Philadelphia, Pa	Mar. 3, 1863	37,807
Armor-plates, Mode of protecting	M. Bernabé	Toulon, France	Jan. 15, 1867	61,143
Armor-plates, Pile for	J. Jeavons	Sheffield, England	Dec. 13, 1870	110,143
Armor-plates, Press for bending ships'	E. Sauer	New York, N. Y	Mar. 24, 1863	37,962
Armor-plates to marine batteries, Means of affixing defensive.	O. G. Stillman	Fabius, N. Y	Nov. 25, 1862	37,013
Armor-plates to vessels, Attaching	J. Rusch	New York, N. Y	May 20, 1862	35,353
Armor, Ships' defensive	S. D. Carpenter	Madison, Wis	May 23, 1865	47,796
Armor to navigable vessels and water batteries, Means of attaching.	J. B. Love	Philadelphia, Pa	Oct. 22, 1861	33,532
Armored car	W. F. Thompson	Toledo, Ohio	May 7, 1872	126,502
Armor-plating for vessels	G. J. Gunther	London, England	Nov. 24, 1868	84,418
Army stretcher	J. J. Smith	Philadelphia, Pa	Sept. 8, 1863	39,840
Arrow-spring	J. B. Cleaveland	Indianapolis, Ind	Aug. 15, 1871	118,108
Articulator	E. T. Starr	Philadelphia, Pa	May 19, 1868	78,151
Artillery and mining blasting	T. P. Shaffner	Louisville, Ky	Dec. 18, 1866	60,572
Artillery, Carriage for field	D. Cobb	Boston, Mass	Apr. 25, 1808	....
Artillery carriages, Wheel for flying	J. D. Murphy	Baltimore, Md	Apr. 3, 1860	27,733
Artillery, Field	S. W. Wood	Cornwall, N. Y	May 7, 1872	126,607
Artist's stretcher	J. E. Todd	Middletown, Conn	Sept. 18, 1866	58,154
Artist's stretching-frame	J. F. Carroll	South Boston, Mass	July 21, 1868	80,135
Artist's materials, Apparatus for drying	G. D. Jones	New York, N. Y	Dec. 11, 1866	60,382
Arts, Composition of matter for various uses in the	C. L. Coombs	Washington, D. C	Aug. 24, 1869	94,080
Asbestus and obtaining useful products therefrom, Treating.	J. S. Rosenthal	Philadelphia, Pa	Aug. 20, 1872	130,663
Asbestus and other fibrous minerals, Treating	C. A. Stevens	New York, N. Y	Mar. 14, 1871	112,650
Asbestus and other mineral fibers for useful purposes, Treating	C. A. Stevens	New York, N. Y	Mar. 14, 1871	112,649
Asbestus for the production of textile fiber, Treatment of.	J. S. Rosenthal	Philadelphia, Pa	Aug. 6, 1872	130,245
Asbestus, Treating	J. S. Rosenthal	Philadelphia, Pa	Aug. 13, 1872	130,538
Asbestus, Use and application of	J. Scott	Philadelphia, Pa	Nov. 26, 1835	....
Asbestus yarn	J. S. Rosenthal	Philadelphia, Pa	Aug. 13, 1872	130,537
Ash-bin	W. W. Chase	Springfield, N. H	July 28, 1868	80,451
Ash-box	G. Dunlop	Williamsburgh, N. Y	Sept. 24, 1872	131,607
Ash-box	J. Kee and J. Sloan	Philadelphia, Pa	Apr. 24, 1866	54,179

That the experience acquired during the war should have added largely to every subject connected with military surgery was not to be anticipated. But it may be safely asserted that, in many directions, it has advanced the boundaries of our knowledge. Even in the very difficult field of investigation presented by the wounds and injuries of the head, we have learned something. Surgeons have been schooled to deal with the most ghastly injuries of the face without dismay, to obtain unexpected results, and to accomplish favorably reparative operations from which, formerly, they would have recoiled; and they have been taught the futility of tying the great arterial trunks of the neck for hæmorrhage from face-wounds. The true principles of treatment of wounded arteries in the neck is now generally understood; and while, before the war, there were few surgeons who chose to undertake operations on the great vessels, there are now thousands who know well when and how a great artery shall be tied. Our information respecting injuries of the vertebral column has been augmented; and, passing to the wounds of the chest, we find a complete revolution in theory and practice. Without further illustration, we may claim that the additions to surgical knowledge acquired in the war are of real and practical value.

GEORGE A. OTIS.

Document 36. Excerpt from *Introduction to Medical and Surgical History of the War of the Rebellion,* pp. XXVIII and XXVIX, Washington: Government Printing Office, 1870. [National Archives]

copy No 1533

Head Quarters 2nd Division 3rd Corps

August 26th 1863

Gun, shot wound excision of part of Ulna

A resection of one of the bones of the forearm performed by me at chancellorsville, as I have not seen the specimens since I operated, I do not remember wether it was an ulna or radius. If I remember correctly, it was a minnie ball wound. The wound in the soft parts was enlarged, the loose piece of bone pulled out, the bone clipped off smoothe at one extremity and sawed across at the other, with a metacarpel saw. The wound being brought together with the Silver wire suture. These exsections of portion of the bones of the forearm have, un=iformly in my practice, done well. Amputation of the forearm for Rifle or musket ball wound, should, in my opinion be seldom if ever performed – resection is preferable.

(Signed) J Theodore Calhoun

Asst Surg. U.S.A.

Document 37. Letter from J. Theodore Calhoun, Assistant Surgeon, U.S. Army, August 26, 1863. [National Archives]

No XII

George W. Clark, 1st Sergt. Co C. 30th N.Y.
Was wounded at the second battle
of Bullrun August 30th 1862 by a Minié & and
Musketball, the first of which entered right
ankle, the latter the right leg about two inches
above ankle, completely shattering the bone.
Mortification supervening, the leg was
amputated about 4 inches below knee by
Dr Loring (20th N.Y.?) Sept 4th 1862.
Modus operandi: Flapoperation
Patient was sent to College Hospital
Georgetown on the 5th of September
Treatment: Cold water Dressing,
Poultices, Tonics.

War Department
Surgeon General's Office

Washington City, May _____ 1864

Mr L. Casella

No. 23 Hatton Garden

London. England.

Sir:

I have the honor to inform you that Medical Officers of the U. S. Army are in future to be furnished by the Government with Clinical Thermometers, and to enquire whether you can furnish them, and if so, at what price per hundred.

The style required is a Maximum Thermometer, graduated to half degrees F, so clearly that quarter degrees can readily be estimated by the eye. The graduation to extend from 85° F to 115°, with sufficient room above for expansion to 125° F. Part of them are desired straight, and part

curved .   It is also desirable that
if possible the instrument should not be more
than ten inches long in order that it may be
as strong and as portable as possible . The whole
number required will probably be three hundred and
I wish to know how soon you can begin to furnish
them   I am aware that delay in graduating
the tubes after they have been filled is desirable, and
I wish the instruments to be of first class workmanship,
accurate and corresponding with each other.   I
should also like to have a sample of the instrument
which you propose to furnish, or of any modifications
which you may think proper, delivered to Mr Wm
Wesley by whom this letter will be presented and
who will pay for the same .   An early reply
is requested .

By order of the Surgeon General,
Very respectfully
Your obt. servt.

(Signed) John. S. Billings
Bvt. Lt. Col. & Asst. Surg. U.S.A.

Document 39b. Letter to Mr. L. Casella from Lt. Col. John Billings, May 1864. [National Archives]

"Copy" N° 1681.   Douglas General Hospital.
                              Washington D.C.

Private Philip Fitzsimmons Co E. 2ᵈ U.S. Cavalry
Age 30. was wounded at Brandy Station, Va. August 1ˢᵗ
1863 by a bullet which entered the right leg at its middle
on the outer aspect — comminuted the fibula, and
passed out at the inner edge of the gastrocnemius.

The case did well under ordinary treatment
untill August 12ᵗʰ when there were symptoms of tetanus
developed, There was stiffness of the neck, slight trismus
Towards evening the trismus increased, and became
so decided, that the teeth only could be seperated for
half an inch. There was involuntary twitching of the
muscles of the thigh of the leg wounded causing
great pain, and recurring at short intervals.

The wound was explored with the assistance of
an anaesthetic, and a portion of the fibula was
removed with forceps from the belly of the gastrocnemius
where it had been driven by the impact of the ball,
and where it might have been causing injurious pressure
upon the posterior tibial nerve.

Large and frequently repeated doses of tincture
of opium and brandy were ordered, as there was most
decided nervous prostration, and Ext. Canabis Indᵗ. in
one gr. doses, was given every 2 hours

Aug 13ᵗʰ The large doses of brandy with tincture
of opium and Canabis Indicae lessened the frequency

Document 40a. Case history concerning Pvt. Philip Fitzsimmons,
wounded August 1, 1863. [National Archives]

of the muscular contractions, diminished the pain, and caused deep sleep.

On the 13th opisthotonos was well marked — the neck was very stiff and drawn backwards; the back was elevated above the bed, and was supported by pillows, and the abdominal muscles were in a state of firm tonic contraction.

The pulse was 78 per minute and the respiration 10.

This amelioration of the symptoms, was the only effect of the remedies; for the disease seemed to progress unchecked.

Aug 14th The pulse was 100 and feeble, the skin bathed with moisture, the patient almost insensible, with the stimulants and narcotics, but answering questions when aroused.

It had been necessary to increase the dose of all the remedies, as the spasms recurred with great violence and frequency, when the nervous system was not deeply influenced by the narcotics. The evidence of nervous exhaustion became more marked, as the case progressed, and the pulse rose until it reached 150 and the respiration 30 per minute. The usual symptoms of death from nervous prostration gra=dually appeared, and death occurred at 9 P.M. without any struggle.

The mind remained unaffected throughout, although there was the usual hebetude produced by the narcotics.

The stimulants and narcotics produced

a most decided amelioration of all the symptoms, but no decided effect on the tetanus. The spasms were con‚ trolled by these agents, and deep sleep with its happy anaesthesia, rendered the last hours comfortable.

Postmortem thirteen hours after death.

A laceration in the gastrocnemius and soleus mus= cles was found whence the fragment of bone was removed on the 12ᵃ extending to within a line of the posterial tibial nerve. The trunk of the nerve, however was apparently healthy

The spinal cord was removed, from the base of the brain to the inferior extremity, and was found with its meningeal vessels engorged

No other signs of organic lesion were found.

W Thomson
A. Surgeon U.S.A.

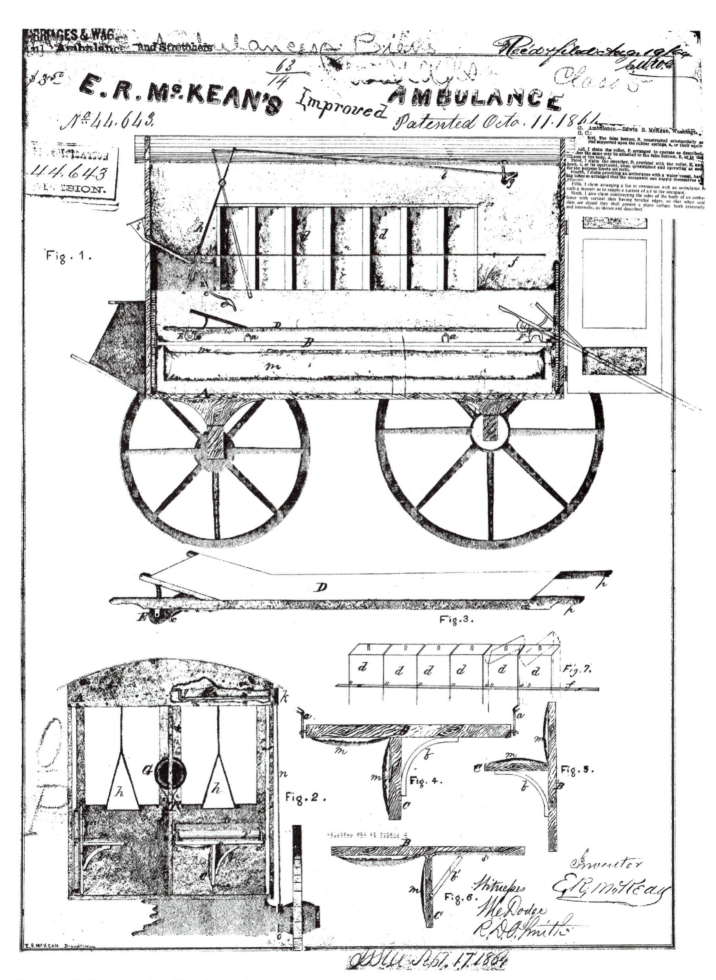

Document 41. Patent drawing, "E. R. McKean's improved ambulance," October 11, 1864. [National Archives]

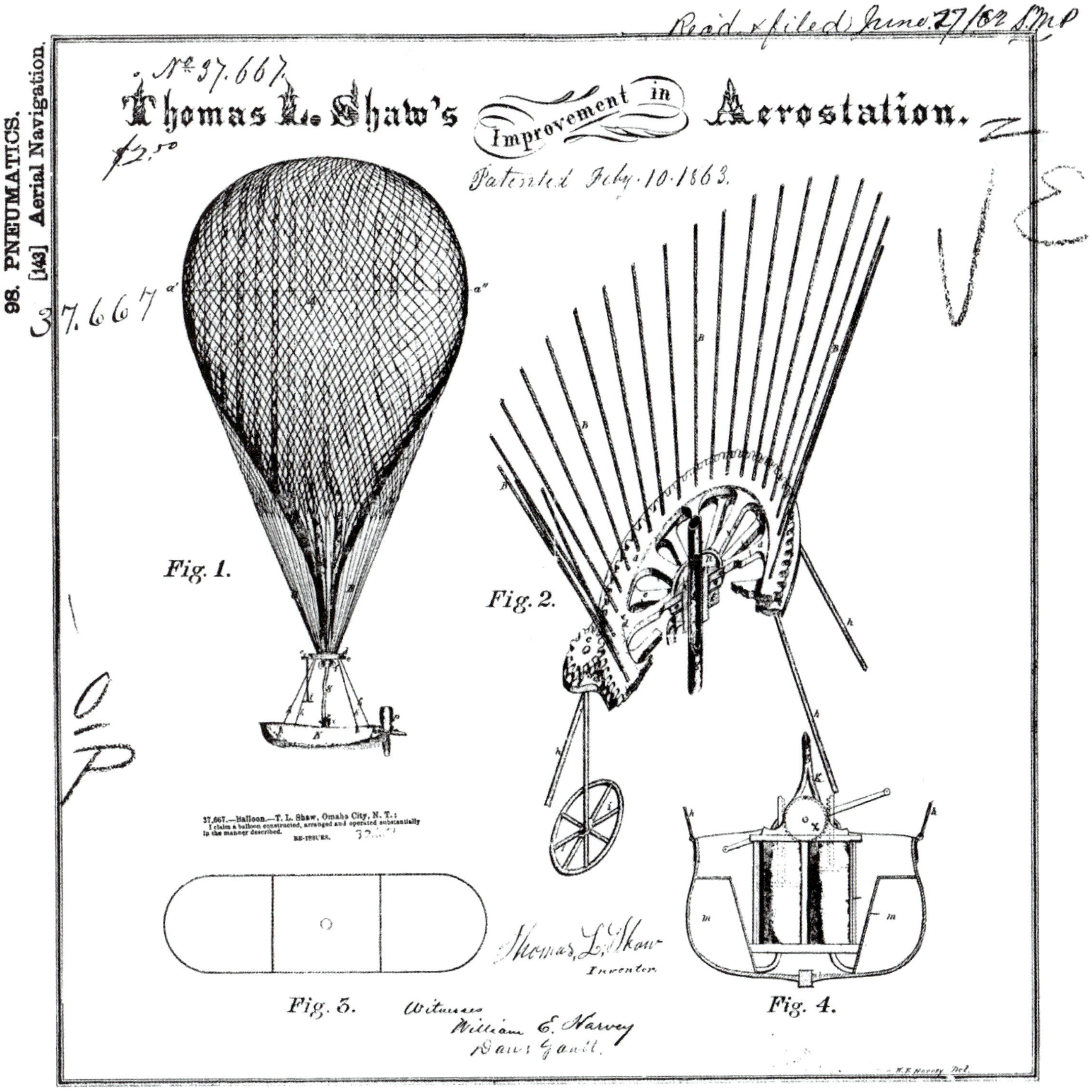

Nº 37.667.

Read & filed June. 27/82 SMP

Thomas L. Shaw's Improvement in Aerostation.

Patented Feby. 10. 1863.

Fig. 1.

Fig. 2.

37.667.—Balloon.—T. L. Shaw, Omaha City, N. T.: I claim a balloon constructed, arranged and operated substantially in the manner described. RE-ISSUES.

Fig. 3.

Fig. 4.

Thomas L. Shaw,
Inventor.

Witnesses
William E. Narvey
Dan: Gauil.

Oct. 15, 1863

H. Lick ✓

Col

Sir

I am directed by the Comdg General to inform you that the suppression of the "Rolla Express" has been ordered and that its Editor H. Lick will be arrested and sent here for trial for publishing articles in violation of S.O. #96. from these Hdqts,

The Chp will be prepared & upon his arrival here you will hold him for trial,

I am Col very respy &c

Col J.O. Broadhead
Provost Marshal Genl

E. W. March
A.A.G.

Document 43. Letter regarding the arrest order for H. Lick, October 15, 1863. [National Archives]

Elizabeth Town Hardin County Ky

Jan 31st 1863

General Boyle

Sir Set my self
down to make a plan statements
of facts to you, Last sept one
year ago The union forces under
Gen, Sherman Camped near My
house and took to the amt of
Three hundred and fifty dollars
worth of provisions &c for which
he gave a certificate recommending
it to be paid when the war
Ceases in Kentucky,

When John Morgan came through
our state in December he Camped
on the Bardstown road near
My farm and fed out at least
700 bu of Corn 1 oat stack worth
at least 40$ and 1 hay Stack 14$
They also stold 2 good mares worth
250.$ and several small things
such as axes bee hives &c, When

they left they drove down and put in my lot 2 broke down mules 2 three year old colts and one old Maro worth about 20$ I have fed them up to this time and were taken from me I suppose by the order of Michal Gore as a man he has employed took them in my absence I hope you will an order so I can recover them as a sort of Compensation for my loss by so doing you will confer a great favor on me

If you wish to know who I am and what Course I have pursued since the war broke out I will refer you to Mr Samuel B. Thomas Henry B. Helm Dr Fenton Geoghegan W. Thomas Samuels or Robert Wintersmith

Martin M Bush

P.S. I forgot to name that they (Morgans men) burnt 5000 rails

M M Bush

Order No. 853

Office of Provost Marshal,
St. Louis, Mo., June 2[?] 1862

To Captain Tunnicliff,

    or any U. S. Policeman;

      You will receive Henry Buster from the chief of City Police, and commit him to the Military prison, — he being charged with hurrahing for Jeff. Davis in the streets of this city on the 2[?]th inst.

By order of Chas. B. Leighton, Provost marshal

W. P. McCracken
Sergt.

    Permit Buster to remain till he pays his fine — Notify the Chief that you have this order immediately.

The Rolla Express.

"RIGHT ON!"

H. LICK. - - - - Editor.

ROLLA, MO., OCTOBER 10, 1863.

The Radical Emancipation &
UNION TICKET.

FOR JUDGES OF THE SUPREME COURT
HENRY A. CLOVER, of St. Louis County.
ARNOLD KREKEL, of St. Charles County.
DAVID WAGNER, of Lewis County.

☞Election on the first Tuesday in November.☜

SOLDIERS AND LOYAL CITIZENS, COME TO THE RESCUE!

For the offices of Judge and Prosecuting Attorney of this (the 18th) Judicial District, there is probably at the present time four of the most dangerous candidates toward the friends of the Union, in the field that could possibly be supported by the common enemies of our country, viz: W. G. Pomeroy, Leet. J. E. Chauvin and Warmoth.— Most, if not all, of these deceitful office seekers have been in open rebellion with the Government and to-day are giving aid and comfort to armed rebels. Will the soldiers and loyal people of Missouri remain quiet and submit to the dictates of brazen politicians whose every acts are marked with conspiracy and sympathy toward the rebellion? Will the soldiers among us who are fighting bushwhackers almost next to our doors stand idley by and submit to rebel sympathizers putting men in office who would justify cold-blooded murderers in all their hellish slaughter among Union men? What will these secession conspirators next stoop to to effect their election to offices where they may wield deathblows for the destruction of the Government? Look at them, in all the disguise the fiends of Hell can put upon themselves, playing the part of Conservatives and pretentional Emancipationists—just as the case may require. This is no time to parley with "Old Constitution" men about their *rights* and *suffrages* for which these candidates demand a hearing. *Give their black hearts the point of the bayonet.* That is the way to elect sycophantic rebel sympathizers to the *low* positions for which they aspire. The loyal people of Missouri are mad and disjusted at political hypocricy. DOWN WITH THE TRAITORS and damned be he who cries "sympathy.

GAMBLE & CO'S CURRENCY.

The "Missouri Greenbacks" (Union Military Bonds) have already become quite as spurious as was a short time ago the "Wild Cat" currency of several of the Western States. This specie of "Greenback" money is no go—it won't pass muster in the rear ranks, nor any other "ranks," unless it is Gamble's pawn-brokers who exchange goods at 300 per cent. advance on their original cost. And these negro-breeders can well afford to barter in "Stale Currency;" they dare not refuse to dicker in pro-slavery money, for fear the Master President of their Bank will "play off" on them. That's what's the matter. But the freemen of Missouri are not going to pay the slave aristocrat's taxes; neither will they receive or pass his shin-plasters. Gamble & Co. may make Missouri bankrupt, but neither they nor all their hordes of rebel sympathizers can make the loyal people of this State *pass them* at par. That has become a settled fact.

"BE YE THEREFORE READY!"

Rumors are flying about our streets continually of Col. Jo. Shelby's invasion. It is stated that the brush nigh Little Piney and for miles around is literally swarmed with rebels from Price's army; and that Jo. Shelby has been discoved with four hundred rebels about ten miles from Big Piney. Our brave soldiers are "cocked and primed"—*to welcome them to gory graves;* so are our Radical citizens—impatient for the conflict. Come on! ye fiends of Hell—death awaits you!

GENERAL ROSECRANS ON THE FREEDOM OF THE PRESS.

The members of the Democratic (Copperhead) State Central Committee of Ohio a short time since applied to General Rosecrans to inform them what regulations prevailed in his army concerning the circulation of newspapers and political documents. The following passage from his reply is distinguished by its plain good sense and manly straightforwardness. It expresses the true doctrine concerning the circulation of political publications in the army:

"As to newspapers, pamphlets, and other publications—none have been or will be excluded on the grounds of party politics. But I do not belong to that sentimental class who weakly and timidly allow *brawling license to tab true liberty.* Hence, when any publication appears among us so *licentious, lying, or traitorous, as to endanger the morality or is likely to impair the spirit and vigor of this army;* I feel bound by reason justice, and duty to my country, to use my authority to prevent its circulation."

A POLICE DETECTIVE ARRESTED.

A Detective in the employ of Maj. O. P. Newberry, under the direction of Capt. Squire, was arrested and placed in close cnfinement, Monday last, for associating himself with a gang of horse thieves. The Capt. with another man, saw the horses stolen and delivered to the detective, who had joined himself with the gang. The horses were to be sold at Rebel Bend on the Gasconade river, which appears to be the Depot for stolen horses.

Monday evening Maj. Newberry succeeded in arresting two of the gang together with others implicated with the party, all of whom are now "rusticating" at Fort Wyman. The name of the Chief of the thieves is Nathan Cox.

☞ Hon. Henry T. Blow will address the citizens of Rolla, at the Court House, next Friday evening, the 16th inst., at early candle light.

Document 46. Excerpt from "The Rolla Express," October 10, 1863. [National Archives]

By the President of the United States of America,

A Proclamation.

Whereas, it has become necessary, to call into service not only volunteers but also portions of the militia of the States by draft in order to suppress the insurrection existing in the United States, and disloyal persons are not adequately restrained by the ordinary processes of law from hindering this measure and from giving aid and comfort in various ways to the insurrection;

Now, therefore, be it ordered, first; that during the existing insurrection and as a necessary measure for suppressing the same; all Rebels and Insurgents, their aiders and abettors within the United States, and all persons discouraging volunteer enlistments, resisting militia drafts, or guilty, of any, disloyal practice, affording aid and comfort to Rebels against the authority of the United States, shall be subject to martial law and liable to trial and punishment by Courts

6261

Martial or Military, Commission:

Second. That the Writ of Habeas Corpus is suspended in respect to all persons arrested, or who are now, or hereafter during the rebellion shall be, imprisoned in any fort, camp, arsenal, military, prison, or other place of confinement by any military authority, or by the sentence of any Court Martial or Military, Commission.

In witness whereof, I have hereunto set my hand, and caused the seal of the United States to be affixed.

Done at the City of Washington this twenty fourth day of September, in the year of our Lord one thousand eight hundred and sixty two, and of the Independence of the United States the 87th.

Abraham Lincoln.

By the President:

William H Seward,
Secretary of State.

6261

Document 47b. Excerpt from Proclamation No. 94, President Lincoln suspending the writ of habeas corpus, September 24, 1862. [National Archives]

Special Commission Convened at St Louis
Dec 11th 1863, Under Special Orders of War Dept.
Number 494, dated Nov. 6th 1863,

An entry is made upon the Journal of the Commission of
which the following is a copy.

John Bush — there are no papers before us showing
any charges against this Prisoner. We have his own statement
under oath, and the testimony of James Grier and George
Montel. From which it appears that Bush is 20 years
old; lives in Miss. Co. Mo; is a Farmer; has a mother living;
has but little education; is now and has always been loyal to
the U.S. His mother is a loyal woman; that he was arrested
on the 25th of Nov. 1863, at the house of Mr. Broadacker, who
is a loyal citizen of said Co. and whose son is married to
Prisoners Cousin; that he went to Broadackers on a visit to his
Cousin; that he had no arms; was never in any army; never
was a Bushwhacker, nor engaged in any illegal Service against the
U.S. Government.
He does not know what he was arrested for. We think
that there has been probably some mistake in the arrest of
this Prisoner. We can find no evidence of dereliction
against him. We therefore recommend his discharge upon
his taking the oath of allegiance in the usual Form.

Joseph Hedge told me that he went with his brother John Hedge to I who is a guarilla to Thomas Browns who is a union man for the purpose of Burning said Browns house but they disisted and did not burn it he went with his Brother & other guarillas to the presidential Election on the 8th instant when and where said Guarillas threatened to kill every man who voted for Lincoln which threats detered all the Lincoln men who were present except myself and one other from voting the same Guarillas who was at the polls came the next day in the vicinity of my residence and fired four shots at me I have heard him acknowledge the same facts twice since he has been arrested

Nov 15th 1864

W D Richardson

personally appeared before the undersigned a justice of the peace W. D. Richardson and stated on oath that the fore going is true given under my hand this 16 day of nov 1864

W H Pate J Poe

Document 49. Letter from W. D. Richardson concerning Joseph and John Hedge[s], November 16, 1864. [National Archives]

Louisville Ky Dec 1864

Cap Charles H Fletcher
                    1st U.S. Inf
        Captain

                    My brother
Joseph Hedges was arrested at his house
in Davies County upon the charge of
harboring guerrillers as I understand,
Joseph Hedges is a truly loyal man
and has even been to and is still a
consistant supporter of the goverment,
I have a brother John Hedges who is
roaming about the County in Command
of a guerriller band, and I have
heard my brother John say that he
would just as soon kill Joseph
as any other I recollect John also
said to me when he visited my aunts
house where I was visiting some three or
four weeks since that Joseph should
pay for his Lincolenism by piloting

him all over the green river country
I am sure
I can say that my brother Radolph
was compelled by John to accompany
him through the country. when I saw
John he was on his way to Davies County.
I refer to Mr Joseph Wright who has
been John say Make the remark that he
would as soon kill Radolph as any
Lincolnite. I have a brother Bristor in
the 26 Ky Inf. a cousin John Yunnels
who was a member of the 26 but being
promoted was transferred to some other
Reg— I refer to Dr Jennings
Maj Gen Rousseau were here in the
City. Henry Dent formerly Col in Fall
being pro marches of this City
    Joseph Hedges family consists
of wife and four children two blind
and their circumstances are
such that they cannot live without
the assistance of their Father. If you
can render me any assistance either

by securing a trial for my brother or even ascertaining the particulars in his case you will much relieve my greatly distracted mind and place me under many obligations

Fannie Dent

November 28t 1864 Daviess Co Ky

Col Maxwell I wish your assistance
in this my hour of trouble, having heard
of your kindness in similar cases I feel bold
esolicit your aid and counsel I wish you
try to give my husband a fair trial if you
can have any influence which I doubt not
you have. my husband is a Union Man he is
as much opposed to Guerrillas as you or any
one but he can not help what his Brother does
and I do not know whether he will be allowed
a trial or not I wish you to urge a trial and
I can send affidavits from under the hands
of Union men to clear him of the charges
that are against relying on your assistance
I subscribe my self your humble servan
Livinia Hedges

pleas hand this to Brisco

Oath of Allegiance, Taken by the Officers and Employees of the Hannibal & St. Joseph R. R. Co., Unconditionally, for the UNION in the Past, Present and Future.

Long may it wave.

I, _J. P. Bush_ of _____ County, of _Monroe_ State of Missouri, do solemnly swear that I will support, protect and defend the Constitution and Government of the United States against all enemies, whether domestic or foreign; that I will bear true faith, allegiance and loyalty to the same, any ordinance, resolution or law of any State Convention or Legislature to the contrary notwith= standing; and, further, that I will well and faithfully perform all the duties which may be re= quired of me by the laws of the United States. And I take this oath freely and voluntarily, without any mental reservation or evasion whatsoever, with a full and clear understanding that Death, or other punishment by the judgment of a Military Commission, will be the penalty for the violation of this my solemn oath and parole of honor.

Certificate:

Subscribed and sworn to before me this 3rd day of March A. D. 1862, as witness my hand and Official Seal

J. P. Bush   (SEAL)

Rect B. Moat, Notary Public

Witnesses:

Wm H Baker Hannibal P. O., Marion County, Mo.

Slasher   "   "   "   "

                             "   "   "   "

IN TRIPLICATE.

One copy to be given to person taking the oath.
One copy to be sent to the Head=Quarters of the Department.
One copy to the Commanding Officer or Provost Marshal of the camp, garrison, town or county where the oath was taken; and no oath to be administered except by order or with the knowledge of said Commanding officer or Provost Marshal.

Albany Oct 12, 1861.

Sir

Enclosed you will find several secession articals sent from St Louis by a creature of the worst reputation. She sends them to men here to keep them from enlisting she has the use of a great deal of money, and by misrepresenting things she has a great influence over men that have associated with her, and I think she ought to be under arrest, she can be found at 43 ~~xxx~~ South fourteenth, enquire for Mrs Ann Bush or Mrs Mary Ann Bush or ~~Mrs~~ Blackman or Miss Flynn she formerly came from Albany and has so many aliass that it will be hard to get her right name, she is of medium height dark eyes and hair and dark complexion she looks about 30 years of age

yours in haste

C. Brown

Mrs. Ann Bush,

alias

Mrs. Mary Ann Bush

alias,

Mrs. Blackman

alias

Miss Flynn

_____

Return to Col. R. Harris

Look out for this American. She needs watching.

Our spy man may return himself in a few affairs.

Chas R. Brown

Charges and Specifications preferred against H. Lick, a citizen of the town of Rolla, in the county of Phelps, and state of Missouri; and Editor of the Rolla Express.

Charge First

Encouraging insubordination and disorderly conduct among the troops in violation of General Orders No. 96, of 1863, from Head Quarters Department of the Missouri.

Specification; In this that he H. Lick, a resident of the town of Rolla, in the county of Phelps, State of Missouri, and editor of a Newspaper published in said town of Rolla, under the name of "The Rolla Express," did on or about the tenth day of October, eighteen hundred and sixty three, write and publish or cause to be published in said newspaper An article under the title or caption of "Soldiers and loyal citizens come to the rescue," which said article was calculated, designed and intended by the said Lick, to encourage insubordination and disorderly conduct, among the troops in the state of Missouri; which said article so written by the said Lick, and published in the Rolla Express, is in words and figures as follows, to wit;—

Document 54. Excerpt from charges and specifications against H. Lick, October 10, 1863. [National Archives]